A Time and a Place

Remember Aldeburgh when you read this rather odd poet, for he belongs to the grim little place and through it to England.

E.M. Forster

A Time and a Place

George Crabbe,
Aldeburgh and Suffolk

Frances Gibb

The Lutterworth Press

The Lutterworth Press

P.O. Box 60
Cambridge
CB1 2NT
United Kingdom

www.lutterworth.com
publishing@lutterworth.com

Paperback ISBN: 978 0 7188 9611 9
PDF ISBN: 978 0 7188 9612 6
ePub ISBN: 978 0 7188 9613 3

British Library Cataloguing in Publication Data
A record is available from the British Library

First published by The Lutterworth Press, 2022

Copyright © Frances Gibb, 2022

All rights reserved. No part of this edition may be reproduced, stored electronically or in any retrieval system, or transmitted in any form or by any means, electronic, mechanical, photocopying, recording, or otherwise, without prior written permission from the Publisher (permissions@lutterworth.com).

To Michael David Anthony
in memory

Contents

List of Illustrations   ix

Acknowledgements   xi

Chronology   xiii

Introduction: A Local Habitation and a Name   1

Chapter 1   George Crabbe's Aldeburgh   7
    California: Crabbe recalled   7
    Aldeburgh: A wild amphibious race   12
    Crabbes in East Anglia: Too obscure to possess a history   17
    Aldeburgh: That boy must be a fool   21
    Wickhambrook and Woodbridge: La! Here's our new 'prentice!   27
    Aldeburgh: The Leech Pond   33

Chapter 2   Growing to Manhood:
                  Love, London and Literary Success   43
    Parham: A young lady that would just suit you   43
    London: I have parted with my money, sold my wardrobe   52
    London: The hand that rescued him   56
    Aldeburgh revisited: A prophet is not without honour...   62

Chapter 3   Domesticity and Botanising:
                  Crabbe's Middle Years   69
    Belvoir and Stathern: The very happiest years in his life   69
    Parham and Glemham: A family walk through the green lanes   74
    Rendham: The final Suffolk years   82

Chapter 4   Religion and Politics   87
    Crabbe and religion: Without a little Latin, we should
    have made nothing of you   87
    Crabbe and opium: His long and generally healthy life   92
    Crabbe and politics: We can do no good, or we would
    be among them   97

Chapter 5   Character and Creation   103
    Aldeburgh: I hear those voices that will not be drowned   103
    Aldeburgh: Grimes on the beach   111
    Aldeburgh: Untouched by pity, unstung by remorse   114
    Crabbe and writing: What I thought I could best describe,
    that I have attempted   118
    Leaving Suffolk: The seat of joy, the source of pain   125

Chapter 6   Endings and Beginnings   139
    Bath and London: I am something of a novelty   139
    Crabbe and women: Oh! For some Made-on-purpose-Creature   144
    Trowbridge: A few Sundays more   150

Postscript   161

Bibliography   163

Index   167

List of Illustrations

Photographs are the author's own unless otherwise stated.

1.	E.M. Forster on Aldeburgh Beach *Getty Images*	3
2.	Britten and Pears's copy of *The Life and Poetical Works* *Courtesy of Britten Pears Arts*	9
3.	Job Bulman, Moot Hall and Market, c. 1769 *Courtesy of Aldeburgh Museum Charitable Trust*	15
4.	Graves of Mary and George Crabbe, Aldeburgh Churchyard	15
5.	Bust of George Crabbe by Thomas Thurlow, Church of St Peter and St Paul, Aldeburgh	18
6.	Slaughden, c. 1900 *Courtesy of Aldeburgh Museum Charitable Trust*	23
7.	'The House in Which Crabbe, the Poet, was Born' *Courtesy of Aldeburgh Museum Charitable Trust*	24
8.	John Harris, Lithograph Map of Aldeburgh, published 1790 *Courtesy of Aldeburgh Museum Charitable Trust*	35
9.	Not Crabbe's House: Parham Hall, Suffolk *Courtesy of Britton Images*	48
10.	Pulpit, Church of St Peter and St Paul, Aldeburgh	67
11.	All Saints Church, Great Glemham	79
12.	St Michael's Church, Rendham	84
13.	Lady Whincup's House, Rendham	85

14.	St Mary the Virgin, Parham	85
15.	Maggi Hambling, *Scallop*, 2013 *Photograph by Chris Newson*	105
16.	Peter Grimes on Aldeburgh Beach, 2013 *Getty Images*	105
17.	George Crabbe by Henry William Pickersgill, c. 1818–19 *National Portrait Gallery, London*	138
18.	Monument to George Crabbe, St James's Church, Trowbridge *Courtesy of St James's Church, Trowbridge*	158

Acknowledgments

This book is a product of the pandemic: for some time I had thought of writing about George Crabbe, particularly after leaving full-time journalism at *The Times*. But it was being 'locked down' in Suffolk that gave me the chance – the time and the peace – to tackle the project.

I am indebted particularly to the moving account of the poet's life by his son, also George, published in 1834; Canon Alfred Ainger's insightful *Crabbe* in 1903; the detailed and colourful narrative by René Huchon in 1907; and Neil Powell's compelling biography of 2004. When quoting Crabbe's poetry I have first used *Selected Poems* (Penguin, 2015) as most easily referenced; and then, for those works not included in that collection, the *Poetical Works of George Crabbe* (OUP, 1932).

I owe many people thanks for support and encouragement. In particular I must mention Dr Nicholas Clark, librarian and archivist at Britten Pears Arts; Catherine Howard-Dobson, curator at the Aldeburgh Museum Charitable Trust; John and Mary James, owners of the Aldeburgh Bookshop; Ian Cook, postman and amateur local historian; my cousin, books editor Mark Cripps; writer Harry Cummins; journalist John Dickie; Canon John Giles, Aldeburgh resident; Dick Jeffery, verger of St Peter and St Paul; Canon Nigel Hartley (former vicar of St Peter and St Paul); the Reverend Mark Lowther (former vicar of St Peter and St Paul). Special thanks are due, also, to Jon Idle for his meticulous copy-editing.

Above all, I am hugely grateful to Adrian Brink and Samuel Fitzgerald at Lutterworth Press who were prepared to take on this book and give it a life.

Finally, of course, I owe thanks to my family – especially to my three sons: Tom, for constant encouragement and advice from across the Atlantic; Patrick, for inspired ideas as well as astute criticism; and to James, who spent many painstaking hours editing the book with sensitivity and flair. Throughout lockdown, my black Labrador, Bella, was a constant and comforting companion. And in spirit, my late husband Joe was always with me.

Chronology[1]

1754: George Crabbe born on Christmas Eve in Aldeburgh (then Aldborough), son of George Crabbe (customs official) and Mary Crabbe (née Lodwick).

1762–68: Schooling at Richard Harvey's School, Bungay, and Richard Haddon's School, Stowmarket.

1768: Apprentice to Mr Smith, apothecary and farmer at Wickhambrook.

1771: Apprentice to John Page, surgeon-apothecary at Woodbridge.

1772: Meets Sarah Elmy – his future wife – at Parham, at the home of her uncle and aunt, the Tovells. Engaged later that year.

1775: Apprenticeship in Woodbridge ends. Returns to Aldeburgh and works for his father on Slaughden Quay, then as an apothecary. Appointed surgeon to the poor. *Inebriety: A Poem in Three Parts* published anonymously at Ipswich.

1776: First visit to London. Lives in Whitechapel, attending medical lectures and hospital wards.

1777: Towards the end of the year, Crabbe returns to Aldeburgh and tries to resume practice as an apothecary.

1779: Seminal decision at the Leech Pond to make a career as a writer.

---

[1] Adapted from George Crabbe, *Selected Poems*, edited by Gavin Edwards (London: Penguin Classics, 2015).

1780: Returns to London. *The Candidate: A Poetic Epistle to the Authors of the Monthly Review* published anonymously. Crabbe's mother dies.

1781: Edmund Burke agrees to act as a patron to Crabbe. Crabbe meets Duke of Rutland, Charles James Fox, Joshua Reynolds. July – *The Library* published. December – ordained deacon and returns to Aldeburgh as curate.

1782: April – delivers first sermon in Aldeburgh. August – ordained priest at Norwich Cathedral. November – takes up post as domestic chaplain to the Duke of Rutland at Belvoir Castle.

1783: May – *The Village* published after final revisions by Dr Samuel Johnson. December – marries Sarah Elmy.

1785: Moves in the summer to Stathern, Leicestershire, as curate. Birth of first child (dies soon after). *The Newspaper* published – last published verse until *Poems* in 1807. Birth of son George, later Crabbe's biographer.

1786: Crabbe's father dies.

1787–89: Births of two more children – John, 1787; Sarah Susannah, 1789 (dies in infancy).

1789: Obtains LLB degree and moves in February to the living of Muston, Leicestershire – becoming rector in his own parish.

1790: Prescribed opium for vertigo. 'The Natural History of the Vale of Belvoir' published in John Nichols's *Bibliotheca Topographica Britannica*. Birth of son Edmund.

1791: Birth of daughter Sarah – dies in infancy.

1792: Sarah's uncle, John Tovell, dies and the Crabbes move to Ducking Hall, Parham, where they stay until 1796. Birth of son William (dies 1793).

1794: Becomes curate of parishes of Sweffling and Great Glemham.

1796: Son Edmund dies. Onset of Sarah's mental illness. Moves to Great Glemham Hall.

Chronology

1801–02: Leaves Glemham for Rendham.

1805: Returns to Muston in October – he did not live in Suffolk again.

1807: *Poems* published, including 'The Village' (slightly revised), 'The Library' (revised), 'The Parish Register', 'Sir Eustace Grey', 'The Hall of Justice'.

1810: *The Borough* published.

1812: *Tales* published.

1813: Sarah Crabbe dies. Crabbe falls ill.

1814: Offered and accepts new post of rector at Trowbridge. Briefly engaged to Charlotte Ridout.

1817: First of several visits to London – meets the Hoare family and others in high society.

1819: *Tales of the Hall* published.

1822: Visits Sir Walter Scott in Edinburgh.

1825: Becomes a magistrate.

1828: Meets William Wordsworth and Robert Southey in London.

1832: 3 February – Crabbe dies at Trowbridge after a short illness.

1834: *The Poetical Works of the Rev. George Crabbe* with *Life by his Son* published together by John Murray.

Introduction

A Local Habitation and a Name

Stand on the edge of the wide, windswept expanse of Aldeburgh marshes and look down the miles of estuary towards the sea; linger in the shadowed quiet of the nave of St Peter and St Paul with its irregular stone tiles; or pause by the Tudor Moot Hall – especially when surrounded by market stalls at carnival time – and you are in the Aldeburgh of George Crabbe.

Two and a half centuries on, the town is no longer the rough fishing borough that Crabbe knew. But elements remain – the landscape and the sea, a few of the buildings, and above all the spirit of the place.

George Crabbe (1754–1832), poet, clergyman and surgeon-apothecary, spent most of his life in Suffolk. If, as E.M. Forster said, to talk about Crabbe is to talk about England, it is particularly to talk about Suffolk and the coastal resort of Aldeburgh.[1] Crabbe was born and grew up there – the son of a collector of salt duties on what was Slaughden Quay, before that assortment of dwellings on the southern edge of the town was lost to successive tides.

Even when, later in life, he left his native county and moved inland – ultimately to the softer climes of Wiltshire (where he is buried at Trowbridge) – Aldeburgh and Suffolk remained as an unbroken thread through his writings, the flavour and piquancy that gave his poetry its hard, realistic edge.

[1.] E.M. Forster, 'George Crabbe: The Poet and the Man', *The Listener*, Vol. 25, No. 646 (29 May 1941): p. 769.

Crabbe had a chequered start. On leaving school, he trained as an apothecary's assistant and surgeon, but the family had no funds to support his ambitions. He ended up rolling butter tubs for his father on Slaughden Quay. One day, at a gloomy spot in Aldeburgh then known as the Leech Pond, he decided to head for London and try his luck as a poet. There, by good fortune, he persuaded the statesman and philosopher Edmund Burke (1729-97) to be his patron. It was Burke, too, who encouraged the young Crabbe into the church. A succession of curacies in villages of Leicestershire and Suffolk followed.

But the east coast always stayed with him. As Forster put it: 'there is one other thing about him that we must bear in our minds: his feeling for the scenes of his childhood, for the coast of Suffolk, for the wind-bitten town of Aldborough. He is one of the poets who are never able to escape from their own particular corner of England, however far they travel and however much they read.'[2]

Crabbe's works were consistently gritty – their depictions of destitution and madness often visceral, in contrast to much of the work of the Romantic poets who were his contemporaries. One critic of the day even described his verse as 'disgusting'.[3] Yet it was Crabbe's writing, in particular his poem about the brutal fisherman Peter Grimes who murdered his boy apprentices, that inspired Benjamin Britten's 1945 opera of that name – placing Britten on the world stage, and by association George Crabbe.

Britten is by far the bigger name, the louder voice, of the two men. But both, outsiders in their own ways, were rooted in the Suffolk coastal landscape. Britten had acquired the Old Mill 'in a quaint old village called Snape' in 1937.[4] When he first discovered Crabbe in the summer of 1941, the composer was in California. Four years later, he wrote: 'I did not know any of the poems of Crabbe at that time, but reading about him gave such a feeling of nostalgia for Suffolk, where I have always lived, that I searched for a copy of his works.'[5]

[2.] E.M. Forster, 'Introduction', in George Crabbe, *The Life of George Crabbe by his Son* (London: Oxford University Press, World Classics, 1932), p. xviii.

[3.] Francis Jeffrey, 'The Borough: A Poem, in Twenty-four Letters', *The Edinburgh Review*, Vol. 16, No. 31 (April 1810): p. 36.

[4.] Benjamin Britten, letter to Nell Burra, 14 July 1937. See Donald Mitchell and Philip Reed (eds.), *Letters from a Life: Selected Letters and Diaries of Benjamin Britten 1913-1976, Volume One, 1923-39* (London: Faber and Faber, 1991), p. 495.

[5.] Benjamin Britten, Introduction to Sadler's Wells Opera Guide, *Peter Grimes* (London: John Lane; The Bodley Head, 1945), p. 7.

A Local Habitation and a Name

Figure 1. E.M. Forster on Aldeburgh Beach with Peter Pears and Benjamin Britten, 1949

Crabbe, Britten and other writers and artists – from Thomas Hardy to Ronald Blythe, M.R. James to Susan Hill, and W.G. Sebald to Maggi Hambling with her striking steel sculpture, *Scallop*, on Aldeburgh beach – have been inspired by the place. It has reverberated. And it was just this affinity for Aldeburgh and its environs – first Crabbe's and then Britten's – that fascinated Forster.[6] The landscape, he proposed in a lecture at the first Aldeburgh Festival in 1948, offers a way of looking backwards in time, into both historical and fictional pasts:

> It is with this estuary of the Alde that we are mainly concerned today. It is here, and not on the open sea or the sea-front, that the action of the poem of 'Peter Grimes' takes place. There used to be a little port on the estuary, Slaughden Quay. It was important in Crabbe's day, and was well defined even in my own earlier visits to the district. It is now battered and derelict, and the sea may wash across into it at the next great storm. Here Crabbe worked as a boy, rolling casks of butter about, and much he hated it. Hence Peter Grimes set out to fish. The

---

[6] See Judith Herz, *The Short Narratives of E.M. Forster* (London: Macmillan, 1988), p. 138.

prospect from Slaughden, despite desolation and menace, is romantic. At low tide the great mud flats stretch. At high tide the whole area is a swirl of many-coloured waters. At all times there are birds and low woodlands on the further bank, and, to the north, Aldeburgh sheltering among a few trees, and still just managing to dominate her fate.

I wanted to evoke these sombre and touching scenes as best I could, in order to give a local habitation and a name to what follows. Crabbe without Aldeburgh, Peter Grimes without the estuary of the Alde, would lose their savour and tang.[7]

In other words, Aldeburgh is one of those places that Iain Finlayson, the author and journalist, writing of Tangier, calls 'more a place of the mind than a place in the world; it is an atmosphere rather than a location'.[8] On the cusp of the Mediterranean, poised between Africa and Europe, Tangier has provided both muse and mooring for a wide range of writers (including Samuel Pepys, Alexandre Dumas, Mark Twain, Truman Capote and Tennessee Williams). Aldeburgh – perched on one of the easternmost edges of England – has, in its own understated way, inspired writers, artists and musicians. Its singular atmosphere permeates their works – and their works, in turn, define the town as 'a place of the mind'.

Aldeburgh made Crabbe, but his relationship with the town was always ambivalent. In his introduction to the 1932 edition of *The Life of George Crabbe by His Son*, Forster put it more strongly:

> He hated Aldborough, 'where guilt and famine reign', where his queer rough father had made him roll casks on the quay, where, later on, he had practised as an unqualified surgeon

---

[7.] E.M. Forster, 'George Crabbe and Peter Grimes', a lecture given at the Aldeburgh Festival, 7 June 1948. See E.M. Forster, *Two Cheers for Democracy* (London: Edward Arnold & Co., 1972), p. 167. Forster alludes to Shakespeare's *A Midsummer Night's Dream*, V.1:

> *And as imagination bodies forth*
> *The forms of things unknown, the poet's pen*
> *Turns them to shapes and gives to airy nothing*
> *A local habitation and a name.*

[8.] Iain Finlayson, 'A City of the Dream', *IB Tauris Blog*, 5 December 2014: https://theibtaurisblog.com/2014/12/05/tangier-last-resort-of-the-living-dead/.

and an unwelcomed curate. He compares himself to a swallow, who migrates from the cruel east coast to a happier land. Yet Aldborough dominates his work; it is not only *The Village* and *The Borough* and the parish of *The Parish Register*, but it inserts itself into later poems, and reappears among the quiet inland parsonages and ducal seats of Leicestershire.[9]

Suffolk's influence on Crabbe was not confined to Aldeburgh, however. He spent years in nearby Parham, Glemham and Rendham – some of the happiest of his life. Wandering in the 'green lanes' of these inland villages, he could indulge his passion for botany and insects and absorb the natural habitat. Landscape, for him, was not just a backdrop; it became integral to his characters, often reflecting their states of mind.

Here, for instance, is an autumnal scene that greets a doomed lover looking out from his window:

Before him swallows, gathering for the sea,
Took their short flights, and twittered on the lea;
And near the bean-sheaf stood, the harvest done,
And slowly blackened in the sickly sun;
All these were sad in nature, or they took
Sadness from him, the likeness of his look,
And of his mind – he pondered for a while,
Then met his Fanny with a borrowed smile.[10]

'Surely the most telling impression of the time and the place in our verse', wrote the poet and critic Edmund Blunden in 1947 of this passage, 'perhaps the most ably displayed scene in the poetry of landscape. Yet before the poem's end Crabbe has turned away from that outward scene and acknowledged that his thought had been as much upon the state of mind of his unfortunate hero – the psychological landscape.'[11]

[9.] Forster, 1932, pp. xviii–xix. Variant spelling has been retained here and in other quotations.
[10.] 'Delay has Danger', Book XIII, *Tales of the Hall*, 717–24. See George Crabbe, *Selected Poems*, edited by Gavin Edwards (London: Penguin Classics, 2015), p. 433.
[11.] Edmund Blunden, 'Father and Son', in George Crabbe, *The Life of George Crabbe by his Son* (London: Cresset Press, 1947, originally published 1834), p. xviii.

This book is not just about the facts of Crabbe's life – fascinating though these are. Nor is it intended as a comprehensive biography – they already exist, notably the moving account by the poet's son, also George, published in 1834, that by René Huchon in 1907, and more recently the authoritative life by Neil Powell in 2004. While delving into Crabbe's writings, the book does not attempt an extensive analysis, nor an assessment of Crabbe's place in the canon of English literature.

Rather, it traces the literal and psychological landscapes (to borrow Blunden's phrase) of Crabbe's life – above all, the formative landscape of his earliest years. But the book also looks to events and places away from Suffolk. While Crabbe returned continually to the county of his birth, the map of his life was diverse: Georgian London, rural Leicestershire, later-life dalliances in the west country and pulpit preaching in various settings are all part of that bigger picture. Crabbe's fluctuating fortunes and experiences – the times of his life – offer a foil for the place that was a point of return.

The biography of his son, George, sets the framework for much of what follows. His is the first in a sequence of retellings of Crabbe and his world, whether Forster's lecture or more recent events in Aldeburgh such as the 2013 staging of Britten's *Peter Grimes* on the beach. This book combines the insights of previous biographers with Crabbe's own verses and letters to form a kind of anthology – spanning creative struggle, religious faith, romantic love and opium addiction.

As Crabbe did, the book ventures far beyond the confines of Suffolk – but it comes back, like the poet, to the place that shaped him. It seeks to capture the 'then' of Crabbe's life through the 'now' of Aldeburgh and its surroundings today – through the buildings surviving from Crabbe's lifetime, the monuments that stand to him, and most of all, the landscapes and seascapes he would have recognised. It sets the poet – even at his most cosmopolitan – in the context of the 'local habitation' that gave his poems their 'savour and tang'. And it traces the resonance of the place through the works of writers and artists who have been drawn to this once 'little venal borough' and its landscape beyond.[12]

Aldeburgh 2021

[12.] George Crabbe, letter to Lord Shelburne, June 1780. See Crabbe, *Life*, 1947 (1834), p. 68.

Chapter 1

George Crabbe's Aldeburgh

California: Crabbe recalled

To talk about Crabbe is to talk about England.[1]

When Benjamin Britten read those words, he was homesick and far from England. It was the summer of 1941: war was raging in Europe and he and Peter Pears, the tenor with whom he was to form a lifelong relationship, were in California – both pacificists, they had followed in the footsteps of other English *émigrés* including W.H. Auden and Christopher Isherwood. The arid hot landscape could not have been in starker contrast to the bleak, windswept Suffolk coast of Britten's childhood.

Britten was reading an article in *The Listener* magazine, 'George Crabbe: The Poet and the Man' – the text of a talk given by E.M. Forster on the BBC Overseas Service. It was about the life and work of an obscure eighteenth-century poet who had been born in Aldeburgh, Suffolk – the same part of England where Britten had grown up. It is not known how the composer came across the piece; perhaps it was sent by Auden, a fellow pacifist who was a friend of both Britten's and Forster's.[2]

But what seemed an incidental discovery of Crabbe in California was to be pivotal. Indirectly, it led to a new path in classical opera, putting Britten on the world stage. It also resurrected Aldeburgh's home-grown poet – bringing him to new-found public appreciation and awareness.

[1.] Forster, 1941.
[2.] *A Time There Was*, dir. Tony Palmer, 1979.

It was two years since the composer had set foot in England, and on reading the article he was overcome with longing for the landscape of his childhood. He wrote later, in 1945: 'I did not know any of the poems of Crabbe at that time but reading about him gave such a feeling of nostalgia for Suffolk, where I have always lived, that I searched for a copy of his works'.[3]

Pears found what they wanted in a second-hand bookshop. He wrote to a friend in July 1941 that he had found a 'marvellous Rare Book shop' in Los Angeles where he had bought *The Life and Poetical Works of the Revd. George Crabbe, Edited by his Son* (1851).[4] The copy is now in The Red House, Aldeburgh, where Britten and Pears lived from 1957. Pears inscribed it twice, first in 1978, noting that he had bought it in Los Angeles in 1941 – but then, four years later, adding: '?San Diego?'[5]

Where precisely the book was bought is less important than the timing. Just weeks earlier, Britten had written to a friend, Enid Slater: 'I *am* homesick, & really only enjoy scenery that reminds me of England.'[6] On 29 July, he wrote to the translator Elizabeth Mayer, with whom he and Pears had stayed on Long Island the previous year: 'We've just re-discovered the poetry of George Crabbe (all about Suffolk!) & are very excited – maybe an opera one day…!!'[7]

---

[3] Britten, 1945, p. 7.

[4] Peter Pears, letter to Elizabeth Mayer, 5 July 1941. See Humphrey Carpenter, *Benjamin Britten: A Biography* (London: Faber and Faber, 1992), p. 156.

[5] Dr Nicholas Clark, librarian at Britten Pears Arts, has stated: 'We have that lovely nineteenth-century copy in the collection and Pears inscribed it twice, once in the late 1970s and again in the early 1980s, with the intention of clarifying things. The "clarification" is slightly debatable. […] it leaves us asking whether it was in Los Angeles or San Diego where the book was purchased. We can learn that the volume was purchased by Pears and his writing "we started work" acknowledges that the opera was a collaborative effort. Synopses in Pears' hand confirm his part in building the story at this early stage.' Email to the author, April 2020.

[6] Britten, letter to Enid Slater, 17 June 1941. See Carpenter, 1992, p. 154.

[7] Britten, letter to Elizabeth Mayer, 29 July 1941. See Carpenter, 1992, p. 154. See also Donald Mitchell and Philip Reed (eds.), *Letters from a Life: Selected Letters and Diaries of Benjamin Britten, 1913–1976, Volume Two, 1939–45* (London: Faber and Faber, 1991), p. 961. According to W.H. Auden, the home of Dr William and Elizabeth Mayer in Amityville, Long Island, 'where Benjamin Britten and Peter Pears stayed in 1939–40, [was] a house which played an important role in the lives of all three of us. It was during this

Figure 2. Benjamin Britten and Peter Pears's copy of
The Life and Poetical Works

The *Listener* article, and with it the discovery of the poems of Crabbe, was to prompt the pair's return to England – and to inspire Britten's first internationally acclaimed opera, *Peter Grimes* (1945). In 1964, Britten would reflect on this defining moment: 'It was in California, in the unhappy summer of 1941, that, coming across a copy of the Poetical Works of George Crabbe in a Los Angeles bookshop, I first read his poem, "Peter Grimes"; and, at this same time, reading a most perceptive and revealing article about it by E.M. Forster, I suddenly realized where I belonged and what I lacked.'[8]

What in the piece had so stirred his nostalgia? Forster's article quotes Crabbe describing the Alde estuary with its marsh birds and melancholy mud flats – a watercourse that widens from a small river at the village of Snape over six miles to Aldeburgh, continuing several more miles along the east coast beyond Orford – finally meeting the North Sea.

The landscape is haunting: flat, with vast skies, and often soundless save for the rustling of the breeze in the reed beds and bird calls. Britten already knew Snape – he had bought and renovated the circular Mill House before leaving for the States; it can still be seen overlooking the expanses of reeds bordering the river. In the autumn of 1937, he had wanted a home of his own. Suffolk was the obvious choice – he was born in Lowestoft in 1913 and grew up in East Anglia. He also had some £3,000 after the deaths of his father and mother. The property cost him a few hundred pounds.[9]

Britten fell in love with Snape. When he came back from the States in 1942, he wrote to Elizabeth Mayer: 'Snape is just heaven. I couldn't believe that a place could be so lovely. The garden was looking so neat & intentional, & the house is so comfortable and so lovely to look at – & the view … over the village to the river & marshes beyond.'[10] And it was here, at the disused Maltings overlooking the Alde estuary, that in 1948 he founded the Aldeburgh Festival.

---

period that Britten wrote his first opera, and I my first libretto.' Auden, 'To Benjamin Britten on his Fiftieth Birthday', reprinted in *The Complete Works of W.H. Auden: Prose, Volume V, 1963–1968*, edited by Edward Mendelson (Princeton: Princeton University Press, 2015), p. 66.

[8] Britten, *On Receiving the First Aspen Award: A Speech* (London: Faber and Faber, 1964), p. 21.

[9] See Beth Britten, *My Brother Benjamin* (Bourne End: The Kensal Press, 1986), p. 105.

[10] Britten, letter to Elizabeth Mayer, 17 May 1942. See Mitchell and Reed, 1991b, p. 1049.

George Crabbe's Aldeburgh

But it was not just the evocation of landscape that stimulated Britten. He became fascinated with the psychological aspects of Crabbe's characters, how the poet not only looks at the scenery but, as Forster wrote, 'subtly [...] links the scene with the soul of the observer.'[11]

Of Peter Grimes, the sadistic fisherman depicted in *The Borough* (1810), Forster remarked: 'The criminal Grimes is already suspected of murdering his apprentices, and no one will go fishing with him in his boat. He rows out alone into the estuary, and waits there – waits for what?' By way of an answer, Forster quoted from the poem:

> *When tides were neap, and, in the sultry day,*
> *Through the tall bounding mud-banks made their way ...*
> *There anchoring, Peter chose from man to hide,*
> *There hang his head, and view the lazy tide*
> *In its hot slimy channel slowly glide;*
> *Where the small eels that left the deeper way*
> *For the warm shore, within the shallows play;*
> *Where gaping mussels, left upon the mud,*
> *Slope their slow passage to the fallen flood;*

'How quiet this writing is: you might say how dreary,' Forster drily concluded. 'Yet how sure is his touch; and how vivid that estuary near Aldburgh.'

> *Here dull and hopeless he'd lie down and trace*
> *How sidelong crabs had scrawl'd their crooked race;*
> *Or sadly listen to the tuneless cry*
> *Of fishing gull or clanging golden-eye;*
> *What time the sea birds to the marsh would come,*
> *And the loud bittern, from the bull-rush home,*
> *Gave from the salt-ditch side the bellowing boom:*
> *He nursed the feelings these dull scenes produce,*
> *And loved to stop beside the opening sluice.*

Forster's view of these lines was equivocal – sceptical as to their technical merit and yet arrested by their evocative force: 'Not great poetry, by any means, but it convinces me that Crabbe and Peter Grimes and myself

---

[11.] Forster, 1941, p. 769.

do stop beside an opening sluice, and that we are looking at an actual English tideway, and not at some vague vast imaginary waterfall, which crashes from nowhere to nowhere.'[12]

Crabbe's poem was, as Forster conceded, a powerful mix of psyche and setting: the outcast criminal Grimes is set against and defined through the bleak landscape with its variety of harsh and melancholic sounds. Forster's article would produce its own reverberations – a 'bellowing boom' that passed into Britten's consciousness, and then into his works. 'The reading of this article stirred Ben so deeply,' Pears later said, 'that he felt he couldn't stay in America any more.'[13]

Crabbe, through Forster, had recalled the pair to England and to Suffolk. The discovery of the poet was also a moment of artistic genesis. In a BBC radio programme in 1965, Britten recollected: 'In a flash I realised two things: that I must write an opera and where I belonged.'[14]

Aldeburgh: A wild amphibious race

People speak with Raptures of fine Prospects, clear Skies, Lawns, Parks and the blended Beauties of Art and Nature, but give me a wild, wide Fen, in a foggy Day; with quaking Boggy Ground and trembling Hillocks in a putrid Soil: Shut in by the Closeness of the Atmosphere, all about is like a new Creation & every Botanist an Adam who explores and names the Creatures he meets with.[15]

George Crabbe grew up in just this landscape. He was born on Christmas Eve in 1754 in Aldeburgh (then Aldborough), a small town of a few hundred inhabitants. Slaughden, some three quarters of a mile to the south, was its bustling port. Long since washed away

---

[12.] Forster, 1941, pp. 769–70.

[13.] Peter Pears quoted in Carpenter, 1992, p. 155.

[14.] Britten in a discussion about E.M. Forster with Leonard Woolf and William Plomer (BBC Radio, 11 August 1965).

[15.] Crabbe, letter to Edmund Cartwright, Junior, 1 October 1792. See *Selected Letters and Journals of George Crabbe*, edited by Thomas C. Faulkner (Oxford: Clarendon Press, 1985), p. 50.

by repeated floods, Slaughden survives today only as the site of two sailing clubs, whose moored yachts send out a clinking of halyards on breezy days.

The living in this tiny town on the edge of England, exposed to the North Sea, was hard – as were the natural elements to be contended with. The atmosphere was bleak and rough; smuggling and other crimes were rife.

Crabbe's son (also George) gives a comprehensive flavour of the place in which his father spent his childhood, worth quoting in full:

> Aldborough [...] was in those days a poor and wretched place, with nothing of the elegance and gaiety which have since sprung up about it, in consequence of the resort of watering parties. The town lies between a low hill or cliff, on which only the old church and a few better houses were then situated, and the beach of the German Ocean. It consisted of two parallel and unpaved streets, running between mean and scrambling houses, the abodes of seafaring men, pilots and fishers. The range of houses nearest to the sea had suffered so much from repeated invasions of the waves, that only a few scattered tenements appeared erect among the desolation. I have often heard my father describe a tremendous spring-tide of, I think, the 1st of January 1779, when eleven houses were at once demolished; and he saw the breakers dash over the roofs, curl around the walls and crush all to ruin.
>
> The beach consists of successive ridges – large rolled stones, then loose shingle, and, at the fall of the tide, a stripe of fine hard sand. Vessels of all sorts, from the large heavy trollboat to the yawl and prame, drawn up along the shore – fishermen preparing their tackle, or sorting their spoil – and nearer the gloomy old town-hall (the only indication of municipal dignity) a few groups of mariners, chiefly pilots, taking their quick short walk backwards and forwards, every eye watchful of a signal from the offing – such was the squalid scene that first opened on the author of 'The Village'.[16]

[16.] Crabbe, *Life*, 1947 (1834), pp. 7–8. *The Village* was one of Crabbe's earliest poems, published in 1783.

The contrast with present-day Aldeburgh is stark. These days the town is fashionable and upmarket – with more of the 'elegance and gaiety' that the younger Crabbe noted emerging in the early nineteenth century. Those 'mean and scrambling houses' have been replaced, in many cases, by imposing Victorian villas – often favoured by second-home owners. But Crabbe's own words on holiday visitors could apply now:

> And Summer Lodgers were again come down;
> These, idly-curious, with their glasses spied
> The Ships in Bay as anchored for the Tide, –
> The River's Craft, – the Bustle of the Quay, –
> And Sea-port Views, which Landmen love to see.[17]

Aldeburgh today is sometimes labelled Islington-on-Sea; but that does not do justice to its singular character. Traces of the rawness that Crabbe's son evoked, the imminence of nature, persist. And while it boasts a sailing fraternity, golfers, walkers and birdwatchers, Aldeburgh is not a typical holiday resort: no pier or bustling promenade, candyfloss sellers or slot machines. Its special appeal – the light, the landscape – continues to draw artists, writers and musicians. In their wake come music lovers – fans of Benjamin Britten, obviously, but more widely, devotees of the Aldeburgh Festival and Snape Proms.

The fishing trade has dwindled. A handful of boats still ply their trade and fresh fish is sold from several huts on the beach. The fish and chip shops – two owned by the same family – are famous. But most of the fishing boats lie idle – some carefully restored to preserve the memory of what in Crabbe's time was the livelihood of many of the town's inhabitants.

Beyond the layout of the two parallel main streets, the town would be almost unrecognisable to Crabbe. Landmarks, however, remain: the 'gloomy old town hall', as Crabbe's son called it (now regarded as a charming Elizabethan building – the Moot Hall), and the church, enlarged since his day, on the brow of the hill above the town.

There are few signs to remind a visitor that Crabbe once lived in this place. A marble bust of the poet stands, somewhat hidden, close to the north window in the church of St Peter and St Paul. A street named after Crabbe runs close to the Moot Hall, possibly the street where his father once lived. The Aldeburgh Bookshop, just west of Crabbe Street,

---

[17]. 'Peter Grimes', *The Borough*, pp. 233–37. See Crabbe, 2015, p. 90.

Figure 3. Job Bulman, Moot Hall and Market, Aldeburgh, c. 1769

Figure 4. Graves of Mary and George Crabbe, Aldeburgh churchyard

speculates in its online history that its building is on the site where the Crabbe family house stood – and it might well be, although the present bookshop owner acknowledges that this is hearsay.

But if the town has transformed, the landscape of marshes and mud flats, and the often-turbulent sea, are as the younger Crabbe described. The town is still the victim of regular floods, and coastal erosion remains a real threat.[18] Walk a little way out along the banks of the river Alde towards Snape, across the marshes, and there is no doubt the same atmosphere of timelessness.

From his early days, as E.M. Forster highlighted, Crabbe had something of a love-hate relationship with his home town. In a letter of 1780, he called it a 'little venal borough',[19] and in his early poem *The Village* (1793), he characterised the town's inhabitants as a 'bold, artful, surly, savage race':

> *Here joyless roam a wild, amphibious race,*
> *With sullen woe displayed in every face;*
> *Who far from civil arts and social fly,*
> *And scowl at strangers with suspicious eye.*[20]

For all that he had earlier professed his love of the 'wild, wide Fen', Crabbe was here inclined to depict his habitat as inhospitable. In his contrasting portrayals, veering between beauty and barren ugliness, one can glimpse his ambivalence – his changing feelings about the place that shaped him.

> *Rank weeds, that every art and care defy,*
> *Reign o'er the land and rob the blighted rye:*
> *There thistles spread their prickly arms afar,*
> *And to the ragged infants threaten war;*
> *There poppies nodding, mock the hope of toil,*
> *There the blue bugloss paints the sterile soil;*
> *Hardy and high, above the slender sheaf,*
> *The slimy mallow waves her silky leaf; …*[21]

[18.] Cf. Blake Morrison, *Shingle Street* (London: Chatto and Windus, 2015).
[19.] Letter to Lord Shelburne, June 1780. See Crabbe, *Life*, 1947 (1834), p. 68.
[20.] *The Village*, Book I, 112, 85–88. See Crabbe, 2015, p. 7.
[21.] Ibid, 67–84.

Crabbe left Suffolk in 1805, after fifty years of returning to live in this place. But in his life and work, Aldeburgh and Suffolk remained all-pervasive, whether to alienate or attract. As Forster put it: 'Into the work of Crabbe there steals again and again the sea, the flat coast, the local meannesses, and an odour of brine and dirt – tempered occasionally with the scent of flowers.'[22]

Crabbes in East Anglia: Too obscure to possess a history

Sheltered against the eastern wall of the parish church of St Peter and St Paul in Aldeburgh is a tall double gravestone. The sandstone is deeply weathered, its inscriptions almost obliterated.

The graves are those of Mary Crabbe (1725–80) and her husband George (1733–86), parents of the poet. They lived in Aldeburgh nearly all their lives, where George for many years was a warehouse keeper and tax collector at Slaughden Quay.

The tombstone is the only physical link to the Crabbes' lives in the seaside town three centuries ago. But the church itself evokes their son. The writer Ronald Blythe was aware of walking in the footsteps of Crabbe, the poet, and of time stretching back, as he wandered in the graveyard: 'I would study the lichen on [the] Church tower and on the drowned sailors' tombs [...] It was the exterior of Aldeburgh Church which spoke to Crabbe of immortality – those furry mosses, those botanically cancelled names'.[23]

Inside the church is the sole monument to the poet himself. It is a white marble bust carved in 1847 by the English sculptor Thomas Thurlow (1813–99), who created various church memorials in the locality of his birthplace, Saxmundham.

This posthumous marble portrait imagines Crabbe in the incongruous guise of an elite Roman – his expression pensive, his thinning hair closely cropped in contrast to thick eyebrows, and a toga-like garment draped around his shoulders. The relief carving on the bust's plinth depicts a lyre, an emblem of his poetic calling – and of his still-reverberating voice. Yet, in keeping with Aldeburgh's reluctance to celebrate its famous sons too loudly, the bust is tucked away in an almost-hidden corner of

---

[22] Forster, 1941, p. 769.
[23] Ronald Blythe, *The Time by the Sea: Aldeburgh, 1955–58* (London: Faber and Faber, 2013), pp. 14–16.

Figure 5. Bust of George Crabbe by Thomas Thurlow, Church of St Peter and St Paul, Aldeburgh

the north chapel and is easily missed. Appropriately, the famous stained glass window by John Piper, a tribute to Benjamin Britten, is directly opposite.

Aldeburgh churchgoers were once in the habit of paying homage to Crabbe's statue on Christmas Eve, the poet's birthday, by placing a laurel wreath around his brow for the midnight service – in the style of the garlanded bust of Sir Henry Wood at the Proms.[24]

As for Crabbe's actual grave, it is far away: he is buried in the town of Trowbridge, Wiltshire, where as vicar he spent the last years of his life.

There were generations of Crabbes in East Anglia. But as one biographer has put it: 'Crabbe [the poet] belonged to a family which was too obscure to possess a history.'[25] A number of branches of the name can be traced to Norfolk and, according to Crabbe's son, 'seafaring places on the coast of Suffolk'. It seems probable, he writes, that the first person who assumed the name was a fisherman. Possibly one of the Crabbes of earlier generations was known as Crab and added the 'be' to give the name more dignity. But at any rate, he continues, the Crabbes of Norfolk were for generations 'in the station of farmers or wealth yeoman; and I doubt whether any of the race had even risen much above this sphere of life'.[26]

How did the Crabbes come to Aldeburgh? The link with the quay at Slaughden went back a generation to the poet's grandfather Robert, who was a burgess of Aldborough, with full rights and citizenship of that borough, and (from 1732) a collector of customs at £60 a year.[27] Apparently a man of many talents and business skills, Robert ultimately rose to the acclaimed position of bailiff, or mayor, but less than a year after being elected, he died – in September 1734. His wife Rachel and baby George (the poet's father) were left in poverty. From an early age, the teenage boy had to earn his own living – first as the keeper of a parochial school in nearby Orford. 'In the porch of Orford church, [...]

[24.] Nigel Hartley, 'Introduction', in *Aldeburgh Parish Church, St Peter and St Paul: A Guide* (Leiston: Leiston Press, 2014), p. 5.

[25.] René Huchon, *George Crabbe and His Times, 1754–1832*, trans. Frederick Clarke (London: John Murray, 1907), p. 4.

[26.] Crabbe, *Life*, 1947 (1834), p. 3.

[27.] In 1720, Robert married a widow, Elizabeth Miller, and moved to her home town of Aldeburgh to make his living. She died within six months of their marriage. In 1729 he married a local girl, Rachel Syer. See Neil Powell, *George Crabbe: An English Life, 1754–1832* (London: Pimlico, 2004), p. 2; Huchon, 1907, pp. 5–6.

he assembled the "ragged lads" of the parish, sons of fishermen and of "men who heave coals or clean causeways", and tried to teach them the catechism and reading.'[28] (Crabbe's biographer René Huchon here paraphrases from the poet's own imagining of an unruly school in *The Borough*.)

George soon left Orford to live near other members of the family, at that time in the parish of Seething a few miles north of Bungay, acting as a schoolmaster and parish clerk. But before long he had moved back to Aldeburgh, where he gained a position as a warehouseman on Slaughden Quay. In time, he would rise to be chief Saltmaster – a collector of duties on £10 a year and a customs official like his father, Robert, before him.[29]

The poet's father George was a very young man, not quite twenty years old, when he settled in Aldeburgh. In February 1754, soon after his return, he married Mary Lodwick, the widow of a publican, who was eight years older than him. They went on to have six children, of whom George Crabbe, the future poet – born on 24 December that year – was the eldest.

With Crabbe's father working on the quay, it was probably in Slaughden that the family started life. Nothing now remains of the Slaughden dwellings, washed away by storms and tides over the course of centuries. Still, the modest setting of Crabbe's birth and childhood was critical in determining the spirit of much of his poetry. In the words of his biographer Neil Powell: 'No English writer is more firmly associated with a specific town than Crabbe […] it is ironic that his birthplace and his childhood home should be impossible to locate, demolished long ago and almost certainly now beneath the North Sea.'[30]

[28.] Huchon, 1907, p. 6, paraphrasing from 'Letter XXIV', *The Borough*. See Crabbe, *The Poetical Works of George Crabbe*, edited by A.J. Carlyle and R.M. Carlyle (London: Oxford University Press, 1932), p. 206.

[29.] As Powell notes, 'there is a clear sense of George following in his father's footsteps without ever managing quite to fill them'. Powell, 2004, p. 3.

[30.] Powell, 2004, p. 4. The writer G.K. Chesterton well understood the significance of the small – the local – inspiring the bigger picture: 'The vast Greek philosophy could fit easier into the small city of Athens than into the immense Empire of Persia. In the narrow streets of Florence Dante felt that there was room for Purgatory and Heaven and Hell. He would have been stifled by the British Empire. Great Empires are necessarily prosaic; for it is beyond human power to act a great poem on so great a scale. You can only represent very big ideas in very small spaces.' Chesterton, *Tremendous Trifles* (Mineola, NY: Dover Publications, 2007), p. 122.

Aldeburgh: That boy must be a fool

Let us bear in mind this fact: from his earliest childhood, Crabbe was lulled to sleep by the monotonous and unceasing murmur of the waves breaking on the beach; he chased their light flakes of foam, as other poets have chased butterflies; the only flowers known to him were the seaweed; and all the poetry he saw and heard in nature was the sparkle of the calm sea under a summer sun, and the roar of the surf under the howling of the easterly gales in winter.[31]

Slaughden was once a busy ramshackle village on the spit of land that divides the North Sea from the estuary of the Alde. These days the quay is busy only with sailing and leisure craft. The original dwellings, marketplace and pub – the Three Mariners – were swept away by successive tides: as early as the eighteenth century, the quay had suffered 'great ravages', with the loss of an entire street, and a chronicler in 1909 described it as 'a little sea-wasted hamlet, where most of the few pebble-built cottages have been destroyed by the waves […] the broken walls of ruined houses can be seen half embedded in the shingle of the beach.'[32] The remains of Slaughden were finally demolished by the great storm of 1953.

In Crabbe's youth, the tides would regularly flood the whole town: even now, houses on the front, along Crag Path and in King Street – running parallel just behind – have protective flood boards across their front doors. In the deluge of 1779, the house in which the Crabbe family was living was flooded up to a height of three or four feet. Crabbe's father 'hastily carried a cask of gin upstairs, while his mother, not less eagerly, put her tea-kettle in a safe place', as described by Robert Crabbe, the poet's brother.[33]

The flood became family folklore, with Crabbe's son George later recalling: 'I have often heard my father describe a tremendous spring-tide of, I think, the 1st of January, 1779, when eleven houses here were at once demolished.'[34]

[31.] Huchon, 1907, p. 15

[32.] John Kirby, *A Topographical and Historical Description of the County of Suffolk* (Woodbridge: J. Munro, 1839), p. 145; William A. Dutt, *Suffolk* (Cambridge: Cambridge University Press, 1909), p. 38, p. 44.

[33.] Robert Crabbe, letter to his nephew, 10 May 1833. See Huchon, 1907, p. 20.

[34.] Crabbe, *Life*, 1947 (1834), p. 8.

It is likely that Crabbe and his siblings began life in one of the run-down cottages at Slaughden, close to his father's place of work.[35] 'When my grandfather first settled in Aldborough,' writes Crabbe's son, 'he lived in an old house in that range of buildings which the sea has now almost demolished. The chambers projected far over the ground-floor; and the windows were small, with diamond panes, almost impervious to the light. In this gloomy dwelling the Poet was born.'[36]

The growing family then moved into the centre of Aldeburgh. It is not known exactly where in the town they lived, but they seem to have inhabited the thatched cottage depicted in a print published by Bernard Barton, found in some editions of Crabbe's works and based on an original drawing by the marine artist Clarkson Stanfield RA.[37] (Barton, the Quaker poet of Woodbridge, was a correspondent of Crabbe's and other writers, including Charles Lamb.)

This shows a thatched fisherman's cottage with equipment stored in a shed beside the open front door, a figure resting on the upturned hull of a boat to the left. In reproductions, the dwelling is commonly labelled as the birthplace of the poet. But as Crabbe himself said, in a letter to John, his younger son:

> Bernard Barton's print is of my father's house many years after he left it; never very respectable, it was then a miserable building divided into three poor dwellings. I lived in it, as near as I recollect, on my return from school once or twice, when my father removed into that more southward, where we dwelled some years.[38]

The site of either the thatched cottage or the house to which the family later moved – towards 1770, according to one biographer – is a mystery; but at least one of the homes is likely to have been in or close to the

---

[35.] Powell, 2004, p. 4.

[36.] Crabbe, *Life*, 1947 (1834), p. 4, n. 2.

[37.] Crabbe, *Life*, 1947 (1834), p. 4, n. 2: 'The house [...] was inhabited by the family during my father's boyhood.' In the 1834 edition of the *Life and Poems of the Rev. George Crabbe*, the engraving is subtitled – probably more accurately – 'House of Crabbe's Father'.

[38.] Crabbe, undated letter to John Crabbe. See Huchon, 1907, p. 15. Barton had sent the vignette in a letter to Crabbe dated 26 June 1829.

Figure 6. Slaughden, c. 1900

street named after the poet, near the Tudor Moot Hall.[39] What is certain, though, is that Crabbe grew up amid the rough and coarse hurly burly of the quay at Slaughden. As his son puts it:

> He was cradled among the rough sons of the ocean – a daily witness of unbridled passions, and of manners remote from the sameness and artificial smoothness of polished society. At home [...] he was subject to the caprices of a stern and imperious, though not unkindly, nature; and, probably, few whom he could familiarly approach but had passed through some of those dark domestic tragedies in which his future strength was to be exhibited.[40]

The family was more well-to-do than the mass of the population, but only marginally so. And if the mood at home was stern and capricious, Crabbe was exposed to a decidedly rough-and-ready atmosphere in the town. 'Masculine and robust frames, rude manners, stormy passions,

---

[39.] Huchon, 1907, p. 15.
[40.] Crabbe, *Life*, 1947 (1834), p. 10.

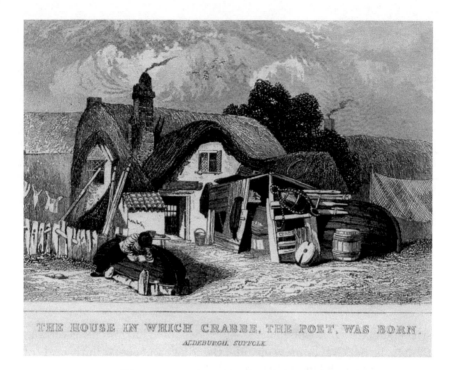

Figure 7. 'The House in Which Crabbe, the Poet, was Born':
Engraving for Thomas Dugdale's England Delineated,
c. 1845, after Clarkson Stanfield

laborious days, and, occasionally, boisterous nights of merriment – among such accompaniments was born and reared the Poet of the Poor.[41]

It had a lasting impact on the young man – and was captured in his most famous writings, including *The Village* (1793) and *The Borough* (1810). He soaked in the myths of Slaughden life and the characters of its inhabitants, creeping into the inns where, 'drawing near the fire, [he] listened to the talk of the customers sitting round the chimney.'[42]

Drawing upon Crabbe's own poems, Huchon vividly reconstructs these early experiences:

[41.] Ibid, pp. 10–11.

[42.] Huchon, 1907, p. 23, basing his impressions on the autobiographical character of Richard in 'Adventures of Richard', Book IV, *Tales of the Hall*. See Crabbe, *Poetical Works*, 1932, p. 359.

Sitting around him were certain personages whom he afterwards described with minute accuracy: as the portly innkeeper, the deep drinkers, boatmen and petty traders concerting a nocturnal venture with smugglers, and, towards the evening, the poor 'dredger', wet to the skin, who tried to sell the fruit of his hard toil. Or he walked along the beach, observed curiously all the refuse and wreckage thrown up by the tide, and now and then went into the cottage of some sailor, whose wife welcomed him 'like a son'.[43]

Wandering today along the narrow spit of land that separates the estuary from the sea, it is hard to imagine this small coastal community. Apart from the two yacht clubs a hundred yards apart, there is an unmade dusty gravel road which runs parallel to the sea wall. The beach itself is marked with groynes and often frequented by families or fishermen sitting along the shoreline. Day trippers park their cars and vans along the slipway for the occasional picnic. This road runs on to the nineteenth-century Martello tower, an edifice from Crabbe's lifetime, beyond which the landscape reverts to the timeless, rural aspect that Crabbe himself would surely have recognised. It stretches on to Orford and beyond, with the sea on one side and river on the other – and little sound other than the coastal birds and the waves.

But despite being born and brought up 'almost within the washing of the surge', Crabbe had few qualifications to be a sailor and was ill-suited to life on the water.[44] His father had a share in a fishing boat and regularly went to sea. He also had a small sailing boat 'in which he delighted to navigate the river'.[45] He often took the young George and his brothers fishing, but 'sorely was his patience tried with the awkwardness of the eldest. "That boy," he would say, "must be a *fool*. John, and Bob, and Will, are all of some use about a boat; but what will that *thing* ever be good for?"'[46]

Even if Crabbe was unsuited to a seafaring life, a voyage in his father's boat was 'the first event which was deeply impressed on [his] memory'.[47] A party of amateur sailors (forerunners of the present-day yachters of Aldeburgh) were assembled to try out the new boat, enjoying 'a jovial

---

[43.] Huchon, 1907, p. 23.
[44.] Crabbe, *Life*, 1947 (1834), p. 12.
[45.] Ibid, p. 11.
[46.] Ibid, p. 12.
[47.] Ibid, p. 11.

dinner prepared at Orford' before a 'merry return anticipated at night'.[48] Crabbe's mother obtained permission for the boy to join the excursion, as described by Huchon:

> They were to sail, as usual, down the Alde, and pass near Orford and the island of Havergate, whose bare, isolated mass divides the river into two arms; farther on they would see, to the right, the green meadows, to the left, the long strip of shingle, the Beach, which dams the ocean on one side and the river on the other. They were to stop for luncheon either at Orford or on the beach, where they could enjoy themselves for part of the afternoon, and towards evening they were to return to Aldborough along the right bank of the Alde.[49]

Crabbe's son offers a more lyrical account of the event:

> Soon after sunrise, in a fine summer morning, they were seated in their respective vessels, and started in gallant trim, tacking and manoeuvring on the bosom of the flickering water as it winds gently towards its junction with the sea. The freshness of the early dawn, the anticipation of amusements at an unknown place, and no little exultation in this father's *crack* vessel, 'made it,' he said, 'a morning of exquisite delight'.[50]

The poet himself wrote about the trip much later in life, in his work 'Infancy – A Fragment', dated 16 April 1816:

> *Sweet was the Morning's breath, the inland Tide,*
> *And Our Boat gliding, where alone could glide*
> *Small Craft, and they oft touched on either Side.*
> *It was my first-born Joy, I heard them say*
> *'Let the Child go; he will enjoy the Day',*

As the sun went down, the men drank copiously ('And growing heavy drank to make them light'), the boys played with the helm and oar, and nervous women had to be set ashore. For Crabbe, in hindsight, the day crystallised into a symbol of how life's events may fail to match earlier hopes and expectations:

[48.] Ibid.
[49.] Huchon, 1907, p. 25.
[50.] Crabbe, *Life*, 1947 (1834), p. 11.

Mid-day it was and as the Sun declined
The early rapture I no more could find.

The promised Joy that, like the Morning, rose
Broke on my View – then clouded at its close.[51]

Wickhambrook and Woodbridge: La! Here's our new 'prentice!

George Crabbe was largely self-taught. Aldeburgh's primary school – a prominent Victorian building at the south end of the town, overlooking the marshes – was not built until 1875, more than forty years after Crabbe's death. He went to one of the local dame schools – places of learning run mainly by women from their homes – and learned to read. From then on, he read voraciously whatever he could get hold of, especially fiction: 'those little stories and ballads about ghosts, witches, and fairies' that 'served, no doubt, to strike out the first sparks of imagination in the mind of many a youthful poet.'[52]

In *The Borough* (1810), Crabbe described such schools with affection and respect:

At this good matron's hut the children meet,
Who thus becomes the mother of the street:

Another matron of superior kind,
For higher schools prepares the rising mind;
Preparatory she her learning calls,
The step first made to colleges and halls.
She early sees to what the mind will grow,
Nor abler judge of infant-powers I know;[53]

But education also took place at home. Crabbe's father would read aloud to the family, in the evenings, from John Milton, Edward Young and other poets. He noticed George's natural talents and resolved to

---

[51.] 'Infancy – A Fragment', 101–105, 120–21, 156–57. See Crabbe, *Poems*, 2015, p. 406–407. Cf. Crabbe, *Life*, 1947 (1834), p. 12, where line 121 is rendered: 'The good found early I no more could find.'

[52.] Crabbe, *Life*, 1947 (1834), p. 13.

[53.] 'Schools', Letter XXIV, *The Borough*. See Crabbe, *Poetical Works*, 1932, p. 205.

educate him as best he could, and 'as that son ever gratefully remembered, was at more expense with his education than his worldly circumstances could well afford'.[54]

Local children also recognised the young Crabbe's scholarly leanings. One day, his son recounts, he was walking home and 'chanced to displease a stout lad, who doubled his fist to beat him', before another boy interfered, saying: 'You must not meddle with *him* [...] let *him* alone, for he ha' got l'arning.'[55]

Crabbe was sent to boarding school on the borders of Norfolk, at the Bungay Grammar School – now Bungay High School. This long-established institution had been founded in 1565. Crabbe was perhaps seven or eight years old. Among the challenges of his new existence was the basic task of dressing himself for the first time. 'The slender and delicate child had hitherto been dressed by his mother,' writes the poet's son. 'Seeing the other boys begin to dress themselves, poor George, in great confusion, whispered to his bedfellow, "Master G ——, can you put on your shirt? – for – for I'm afraid I cannot."'[56]

When aged eleven or twelve, he moved to a school 'of somewhat superior character' kept by Richard Haddon, a mathematician, at Stowmarket, a small town twenty-five miles to the west of Aldeburgh.[57] The sensitive, bookish Crabbe was not unlike the character of the older brother George in *Tales of the Hall* (1819) who 'to a higher class of school was sent, / But he was ever grieving that he went':

> *A still, retiring, musing dreaming boy,*
> *He relished not their sudden bursts of joy;*
> *Nor the tumultuous pleasures of a rude,*
> *A noisy, careless, fearless multitude:*[58]

Crabbe already shared his father's aptitude for mathematical science and it had been decided that he should become a surgeon. He made progress at Haddon's school, but his two years there were not happy, if

---

[54.] Crabbe, *Life*, 1947 (1834), p. 13.
[55.] Ibid, p. 14.
[56.] Ibid.
[57.] Ibid, p. 15.
[58.] 'The Brothers', Book II, *Tales of the Hall*. See Crabbe, *Poetical Works*, 1932, p. 347.

his writings are any guide. In 'Schools', the part of *The Borough* where he evokes school life, Crabbe describes a world where boy-tyrants reigned unchecked:

> *Hark! At his word the trembling youngsters flee,*
> *Where he is walking none must walk but he;*
>
> *Flatter'd by all, the notice he bestows*
> *Is gross abuse, and bantering and blows;*[59]

The indiscriminate violence meted out by the schoolboy moreover echoes the behaviour of Crabbe's famous character, Peter Grimes, in an earlier chapter of *The Borough* ('He wished for One to trouble and control; / He wanted some obedient Boy to stand / And bear the blow of his outrageous hand').

These observations of school life probably originated, partly at least, in Crabbe's childhood experiences. But whatever climate of fear may have prevailed, Crabbe – the 'weaker boy' of 'Schools' whose 'trembling body has the prouder mind' – learned some basic grammar and some easy pages from Latin authors. These later stood him in good stead when he pursued his classical studies and the taking of holy orders. His schooling, however, as for most children, was short and cursory. He left in 1768, in his fourteenth year.

It was a few months before an opening as a surgeon's apprentice could be found. Crabbe had time on his hands and would spend hours in long walks along the Suffolk shore. Again, lines from *Tales of the Hall* could be autobiographical. In 'Adventures of Richard', the eponymous narrator is recounting his early life, pursuits, associations and feelings:

> *I loved to walk where none had walk'd before,*
> *About the rocks that ran along the shore;*
> *Or far beyond the sight of men to stray,*
> *And take my pleasure when I lost my way;*
> *For then 'twas mine to trace the hilly heath,*
> *And all the mossy moor that lies beneath:*
> *Here had I favourite stations, where I stood*
> *And heard the murmurs of the ocean-flood,*
> *With not a sound beside, except when flew*

[59.] 'Schools', Letter XXIV, *The Borough*. See Crabbe, *Poetical Works*, 1932, p. 209. Cf. Huchon, 1907, p. 31.

> *Aloft the lapwing, or the gray curlew,*
> *Who with wild notes my fancied power defied,*
> *And mock'd the dreams of solitary pride.*[60]

Meanwhile, pending an apprenticeship, Crabbe's father employed his son in the warehouse on Slaughden Quay, 'in labours which he abhorred, though he in time became tolerably expert in them; such as piling up butter and cheese'.[61]

His father eventually spotted an advertisement – 'Apprentice wanted' – and Crabbe was offered the post at Wickhambrook, a small village near Bury St Edmunds. This too was not a particularly happy time. When he arrived, having crossed the countryside under the care of two farmers, exhausted and wearing 'a very ill-made scratch wig', he was greeted with hilarity by his new master's daughters: 'La! Here's our new 'prentice.'[62]

Crabbe's new master was an apothecary and the young man learned how to 'bleed'. But as well as apothecary duties, he was employed on the farm where he was the bedfellow and companion of the plough boy – a situation the future poet found utterly demeaning. In 1781, he would recall of his two-year stint at Wickhambrook: 'there was indeed no other Distinction made between the Boy at the Farm and myself but that he was happy in being an annual Servant & I was bound by Indentures'. As a result, he says: 'I rebelled in my Servitude, for it became grievous'.[63]

The experience highlights what Neil Powell has characterised as 'the unbridgeable gulf between those who work by the sea and the river, on the coastal strip of Suffolk, and those who work on the land, inland'.[64] Powell cites the more recent account of writer Ronald Blythe, whose own childhood was spent in inland East Anglia and who has described the sense of semi-alienation he felt when he came to live on the Suffolk coast: 'I found myself in a different state by the sea; not freed, but in another kind of captivity. I lived by it briefly when I first became a writer and felt myself both in my own deeply rooted country and on the edge

---

[60] 'Adventures of Richard', Book IV, *Tales of the Hall*. See Crabbe, *Poetical Works*, 1932, p. 359.

[61] Crabbe, *Life*, 1947 (1834), p. 17.

[62] Ibid.

[63] Letter to Edmund Burke, 26 June 1781. See Crabbe, *Letters*, 1985, p. 9. The so-called Bunbury Letter was sent to Burke, and by him to Sir Charles Bunbury, who was interested in Crabbe's welfare.

[64] Powell, 2004, p. 19.

of things.' Blythe found that his mentality changed in tandem with the landscape: 'The entire ecology changes long before one even suspects the presence of the Suffolk sea.'[65]

Whether Crabbe in the days of his apprenticeship craved the coast or not, he certainly disliked his position on the farm. He later recalled how his father 'was informed of his Son's Idleness and Disobedience; he came & was severe in his Correction of them'. Crabbe, in his own words, then 'became obstinate' with the result that his father took him away and placed him in 1771 'with a man of large business in a more reputable line'. This was John Page, a surgeon at Woodbridge, seventeen miles south of Aldeburgh. The boy's main tasks were 'putting up Prescriptions and compounding Medicines [...] for in 1816 no Pains were taken to give me an Idea of the profession I was to live by'.[66]

And yet these lowly stations were the genesis of Crabbe's life as a writer. As a distraction from the drudgery on the farm and subsequently at Woodbridge, he read novels and poetry and started to write verse, which he contributed to magazines and journals. Even before leaving the farm, he had 'filled a drawer with verses'.[67] Later in life, in an autobiographical sketch penned in the third person, he would recall how he 'wrote upon every occasion, and without occasion; and, like greater men, and indeed like almost every young versifier, he planned tragedies and epic poems, and began to think of succeeding in the highest line of composition, before he had made one good and commendable effort in the lowest'.[68]

In 1772, in his eighteenth year, he had his first literary success with a poem entitled 'Hope', winning a prize offered by the *Lady's Magazine*, published by John Wheble as an 'entertaining companion for the fair sex'. The poem, which proclaims Crabbe's creative ambition, concludes:

> *But, above all, the POET owns thy powers –*
> *HOPE leads him on, and every fear devours;*
> *He writes, and, unsuccessful, writes again,*
> *Nor thinks the last laborious work in vain;*

[65.] Ronald Blythe, *Talking about John Clare* (Nottingham: Trent Editions, 1999), p. 20. Cf. Powell, 2004, pp. 19–20. Blythe's long association with Aldeburgh culminated in his *Aldeburgh Anthology* of 1972.
[66.] Letter to Edmund Burke, 26 June 1781. See Crabbe, *Letters,* 1985, pp. 9–10.
[67.] Crabbe, *Life,* 1947 (1834), p. 20.
[68.] Crabbe, 'Biographical Account of George Crabbe', *New Monthly Magazine,* Vol. 4 (January 1816): p. 512.

> *New schemes he forms, and various plots he tries,*
> *To win the laurel, and possess the PRIZE.*[69]

In his later account of his life, Crabbe would ruefully admit that this early accolade went to his head: 'he felt himself more elevated above the young men his companions, who made no verses, than it is to be hoped he has done at any time since'.[70] He had four other pieces published in the magazine in 1772.

By the time he left Woodbridge after some four years, Crabbe had 'found courage and means (the latter I know not how)', his son relates, to print and publish at Ipswich a short piece entitled 'Inebriety, a Poem'. This three-part work was printed and sold in 1775 by C. Punchard, Bookseller, in the Butter Market, Ipswich, for one shilling and sixpence.[71]

The poem describes how in the middle of winter, with howling winds and sharp air, labourers sit in the warm inn beside the 'dull embers' and listen to tales. Crabbe writes with insight – no doubt experience too – into the distortive power of drink:

> *In various forms the madd'ning spirit moves,*
> *This drinks and fights, another drinks and loves.*
> *A bastard zeal, of different kinds it shows,*
> *And now with rage, and now religion glows:*
> *The frantic soul bright reason's path defies,*
> *Now creeps on earth, now triumphs in the skies;*
> *Swims in the seas of error, and explores,*
> *Through midnight mists, the fluctuating shores;*[72]

Crabbe returned to Aldeburgh towards the end of 1775, hoping to find the means to go to London and complete his professional medical education. But, as his son explains, domestic circumstances blocked his path. There were simply no funds and he was needed at home:

> The Saltmaster's affairs, however, were not in such order that he could at once gratify his son's inclination in this respect; neither could he afford to maintain him at home in idleness;

[69.] These final six lines are the only part of the poem (or of any of the contributions to Wheble's *Lady's Magazine*) quoted by Crabbe's son. Crabbe, *Life*, 1947 (1834), p. 19..

[70.] Crabbe, 1816, p. 512.

[71.] Crabbe, *Life*, 1947 (1834), p. 22.

[72.] Crabbe, *Poetical Works*, 1932, p. 3.

and the young man, now accustomed to far different pursuits and habits, was obliged to return to the labours of the warehouse on Slaughden quay.[73]

Crabbe was back to being 'shouldered about in the cold by rough fellows and learning the smell of things'.[74] The trials of his apprenticeships had landed him back precisely where he had started. And yet, in the years since he moved inland, Crabbe had become at least a novice poet – and begun to absorb those aspects of the world ('the smell of things') that would animate his writing.

Aldeburgh: The Leech Pond

The first glimpse of the sea on approaching Aldeburgh comes as one passes the flint church of St Peter and St Paul, with its fourteenth-century tower – just where the road begins its descent into the town. Somewhere to the right of this approach, in Crabbe's day, was an area known as the Marsh Hill, where there was a muddy pool called the Leech Pond.[75]

Some accounts suggest that this local feature was further north up the coast, towards Thorpeness. But there is evidence that it was in Aldeburgh itself. What is now Park Lane and its environs were once described as the Town Marsh Hill (as recorded by an eighteenth-century map in the Aldeburgh Museum), an area slightly raised above the marshes to the north and south.

Wherever it lay, the Leech Pond marked a pivotal moment in Crabbe's life. As he stood before its mud-clouded water in the course of a walk, he experienced a life-changing epiphany. The poet's son describes the event, according to his father's account:

> One gloomy day, towards the close of the year 1779, he had strolled to a bleak and cheerless part of the cliff above Aldborough, called "The Marsh Hill", brooding, as he went, over the humiliating necessities of his condition, and plucking every now and then, I have no doubt, the hundredth

---

[73.] Crabbe, *Life*, 1947 (1834), p. 26.
[74.] Powell, 2004, p. 32, citing Neville Blackburne, *The Restless Ocean: The Story of George Crabbe, the Aldeburgh Poet, 1754–1832* (Lavenham: Terence Dalton), p. 51.
[75.] Huchon, 1907, p. 81, n. 4: 'It was, I believe, on the right of the road as one goes down to the beach.'

specimen of some common weed. He stopped opposite a shallow, muddy piece of water, as desolate and gloomy as his own mind, called the Leech-Pond, and 'it was while I gazed on it' – he said to my brother and me, one happy morning – 'that I determined to go to London and venture all.'[76]

In his lecture at the first Aldeburgh Festival in 1948, E.M. Forster evoked the moment in more dramatic terms:

> One grim day in the winter of 1779, he walked to the bleak and cheerless Marsh Hill, gazed at a muddy stretch of water called the Leech Pond, and decided to clear out. Leaving 'these shores where guilt and famine reign', he set out to seek his fortune in London as a poet.[77]

The decision had not been a sudden one. In 1775, at the end of his apprenticeship in Woodbridge, Crabbe was back in Aldeburgh, working on the quay, where his tasks included rolling barrels of salt and piling up casks of butter and cheese. He went 'sullen and angry to his work', and 'violent quarrels ensued between him and his father'. Later, he confessed that such behaviour was 'unjustifiable'.[78]

As he toiled, Crabbe's family situation was changing for the worse. His mother, several years older than his father, was an invalid, suffering from the dropsy – or oedema – and his father had taken to drink. In 1774, the year before his return, there had been a contested election at Aldeburgh and the Whig candidate, Charles Long, found an able and zealous agent in Crabbe senior. Political meetings and machinations

---

[76.] Crabbe, *Life*, 1947 (1834), p. 37.

[77.] See Forster, 1972 (1948), p. 167. Forster had been invited by Britten to give the lecture when he stayed with Britten and Pears at Crag House (he told his friend William Plomer that his hosts were 'the sweetest people'). He went on to enjoy a long association with Aldeburgh, taking part in the bicentenary celebrations for Crabbe in 1954, during which the Earl of Stradbroke unveiled a plaque at Lady Whincup's House, Rendham (see p. 83 below). In 1956, Forster gave another lecture at the Festival, entitled 'Alexandria: A History and a Guide'.

[78.] Crabbe, *Life*, 1947 (1834), pp. 26–27.

Figure 8. John Harris, lithograph map of Aldeburgh, published 1790

probably led to more time spent in the pub. In any case, it was from this period that the family dated the loss of domestic comfort, and on the part of Crabbe's father:

> a rooted taste for the society of the tavern, and such an increase in the violence of his temper that his meek-spirited wife, now in poor health, dreaded to hear his returning footsteps. If the food prepared for his meal did not please his fancy, he would fling the dishes about the room, and all was misery and terror. George was the chief support of his afflicted mother – her friend and her physician.[79]

In his effort to care for his mother, Crabbe would catch small fish called butts – the only thing for which she had an appetite for her nightly meal. As Crabbe wrote in 1781 to Edmund Burke: 'my father had a large family, a little Income, and no Oeconomy'.[80] It was a laconic summary of a desperate situation.

His father's decline fed ultimately into Crabbe's portrayals of compromised, troubled characters – perhaps in particular Peter Grimes. As Huchon put it in his 1907 biography:

> When in later life he wished to depict the insensible deterioration of a mind ravaged by vice, he must sometimes have thought of the father from whom he had inherited his energy and his intellectual strength, but whom he had seen a prey to the degradation of drink. He had witnessed heart-rending, well-nigh tragic scenes, caused by drunkenness, in his own family and among his neighbours.[81]

Crabbe senior had been a pillar of the local parish church, St Peter and St Paul. But about this time, in 1775, he gave up being churchwarden, a position he had held since 1768.[82] Instead, the old man became – and remained, for his son – an example of those 'men of masculine and robust frames, rude manners, stormy passions' who dwelt in Aldeburgh

---

[79] Ibid, p. 27.
[80] Letter to Edmund Burke, 26 June 1781. See Crabbe, *Letters*, 1985, p. 9.
[81] Huchon, 1907, p. 20.
[82] Alfred Ainger, *Crabbe: English Men of Letters* (London: Macmillan, 1903), p. 11.

and would later populate *The Borough* (1810).[83] In Huchon's more lurid account, this class of fishermen and workers 'spent their days in toil, and their nights occasionally in noisy orgies'.[84]

So developed Crabbe's ambivalent relationship with Aldeburgh, where, as E.M. Forster observed, he 'grew to manhood in straitened circumstances'.[85] Crabbe's gradual antipathy towards his father, as the latter declined into violence and dissipation, evolved in parallel with his sense of the place and its people.

Then, one day, an old Woodbridge friend of Crabbe's, now a budding young surgeon, came to Aldeburgh to visit his old drinking pal. William Springall Levett was directed to the quay at Slaughden where he was horrified to discover Crabbe employed in menial work and in the dress of a common warehouseman.

Levett commanded Crabbe follow him to the nearby inn (probably The Three Mariners at Slaughden – the sign from which is still to be found in the Moot Hall Museum), where 'he was treated with a long and angry lecture, inculcating pride and rebellion'. In the end, however, Crabbe was subdued rather than provoked by his friend's tirade: he bore it out 'in sad silence' but 'refused to take any steps in opposition to his father's will'.[86]

Nonetheless, Levett's words may have had some effect in persuading Crabbe to pursue a career as an apothecary. He began to look for a position as an assistant, possibly in the shop of James Maskill, who had recently started business in the town. One of two apothecaries in Aldeburgh at the time, Maskill was far from a role model. Renowned as 'an overbearing brutal man, of scandalous conduct', he had only recently started his business when suddenly he decided to leave Aldeburgh for another town.[87] It seemed like an opportunity for Crabbe: he was encouraged by his father and others to take on the practice. Maskill's enemies, too, invited Crabbe to 'fix there immediately'.[88] He duly bought the shop and its stock of drugs on credit.

---

[83] Crabbe, *Life*, 1947 (1834), p. 10.
[84] Huchon, 1907, p. 20.
[85] Forster, 1972 (1948), p. 167.
[86] Crabbe, *Life*, 1947 (1834), p. 28.
[87] Huchon, 1907, p. 63, quoting an entry in the Minute Book of the Aldeburgh Board of Guardians of 17 September 1775.
[88] Letter to Edmund Burke, 26 June 1781. See Crabbe, *Letters*, 1985, pp. 10–11.

About the same time, Crabbe also secured the work of serving the poor of the town from his rival apothecary, Burham Raymond, who 'had the better practice in the place' but had become embroiled in a dispute with the parish. Raymond and the parish could not agree on fees for this responsibility and so in September 1775, the young Crabbe was warmly recommended by his father to take on the job instead, with the stipulation from the Aldeburgh Board of Guardians that he 'be employed to cure the boy Howard of the Itch, and that, whenever any of the poor shall have occasion for a surgeon, the overseers shall apply to him for that purpose'.[89]

And so Crabbe found himself an apothecary and town surgeon. It must have seemed as though his fortune had indeed turned. But subsequent events cast a rather different light, and in his later letter to Burke, he would admit with hindsight: 'an unlucky Opportunity offer'd itself at Aldboro'.[90]

Crabbe's qualifications to practise medicine were extremely limited. He set about trying to improve his knowledge of anatomy and physiology, reading medical books written in Latin. There were opportunities for more practical, visceral experiments in the form of dead dogs thrown up by the sea – apt samples for anatomical dissection. Meanwhile he continued to walk along the shore in search of plants and tiny insects. His interest in botany grew as he collected and analysed local flora such as the 'blue bugloss', the 'slimy mallow' with its 'silky leaf', the charlock, and the tare.[91]

He recalled of this time: 'I read much, collected Extracts & translated Latin Books of physic with a view of double Improvement: I studied the *Materia Medica*, & made some progress in Botany; I dissected dogs and fancied myself an Anatomist, quitting entirely Poetry Novels & Books of Entertainment.'[92]

Crabbe's love of botany and natural history had developed during his stay at Woodbridge, 'the neighbourhood of which had a Flora differing from that of the bleak coast country of Aldeburgh'.[93] Through to his later years, these were interests that Crabbe 'cultivated with fond zeal, both

---

[89]. Huchon, 1907, pp. 63–64.
[90]. Letter to Edmund Burke, 26 June 1781. See Crabbe, *Letters*, 1985, p. 10.
[91]. Huchon, 1907, p. 65. Cf. *The Village*, Book I, 71–76: Crabbe, *Poems*, 2015, p. 7.
[92]. Letter to Edmund Burke, 26 June 1781. See Crabbe, *Letters*, 1985, p. 11.
[93]. Ainger, 1903, p. 14.

in books and in the fields'.[94] His evocation of the fenland landscape in his later poem 'The Lover's Journey' (*Tales*, 1812) reflects his fascination with nature:

> *The few dull flowers that o'er the place are spread,*
> *Partake the nature of their fenny bed;*
> *Here on its wiry stem, in rigid bloom,*
> *Grows the salt lavender that lacks perfume;*
> *Here the dwarf sallows creep, the septfoil harsh,*
> *And the soft slimy mallow of the marsh;*
> *Low on the ear the distant billows sound,*
> *And just in view appears their stony bound;*
> *No hedge nor tree conceals the glowing sun,*
> *Birds, save a watery tribe, the district shun,*
> *Nor chirp among the reeds where bitter waters run.*[95]

For a year, probably from the autumn of 1775, Crabbe spent much time walking through the Suffolk countryside. Along the coast, the sandlings or the estuary, he searched for plants that he would pluck and bring home to identify and catalogue, or sought out beetles and other insects. He would linger on the beach or mud flats at low tide to examine the 'sea-wrack', 'sea-nettles' and other organisms which 'science knows not where to place'.[96]

But despite the fascination of his natural surroundings, Crabbe felt the lure of the city. He knew that he would need to go to London if he were to obtain anything like the medical knowledge required to advance his profession. In late 1776, he left his new apothecary practice in the care of a neighbouring surgeon, and at Slaughden – scene of his former drudgery – he embarked on one of the trading vessels bound for London's East End.

[94.] Crabbe, *Life*, 1947 (1834), p. 26.
[95.] 'The Lover's Journey', Tale X, *Tales*, 118–128. See Crabbe, *Poems*, 2015, p. 234.
[96.] Huchon, 1907, p. 66. Cf. 'Amusements', Letter IX, *The Borough*, 82–86, 89–90: Crabbe, *Poetical Works*, 1932, p. 144. In asserting that Crabbe probably spent the end of 1776 and the first six months of 1777 in London, Huchon corrects the son's chronology of events.

There he stayed with an Aldeburgh family, 'humble tradespeople' who were living in Whitechapel, and he remained for some eight months.[97] Crabbe's hope was to walk the hospitals, attend medical lectures and pick up surgical knowledge as cheaply as he could. In reality, he did not have the funds to get by.

Little is recorded of this first stint in London, save for one strange and horrifying incident. At that time, the new science of anatomy had led to a proliferation in dissection. Corpses were in short supply and the grim industry of 'resurrectionists' or body-snatchers had flourished. Crabbe, like many others, seems to have been willing to avail himself of the corpse industry in order to further his studies. It so happened that his landlady had recently lost one of her children. When she discovered that Crabbe had a dead child stowed in his cupboard for the purposes of dissection, she concluded in her grief that it was the body of her own infant. Crabbe, she alleged, had 'dug up William' and should be brought before the Lord Mayor at the Mansion House.[98]

Luckily for Crabbe, he had not started work on the body and it could be proved not to be the landlady's William. He was exonerated and makes no comment about the episode; but his narrow escape from being condemned as a resurrectionist must have left its mark.

By mid 1776, Crabbe's money was exhausted, his aspirations curtailed, and he was little the wiser in medical knowledge. He had no option but to return to Aldeburgh. Here, he discovered with dismay that the locum to whom he had entrusted his practice had conspired with his rival Raymond to cheat him out of his clientele. Now he was bereft of his business and still lacking in manual experience or diagnostic skills. The second woman he attended in childbirth died less than a month afterwards. Crabbe was probably blameless, but it nonetheless shook his confidence.

Nor did the townsfolk have much regard for him, and his passion for botany did not help. He would return from walks with handfuls of plants which, as they saw it, suggested that 'as Dr Crabbe got his medicines in the ditches, he could have little claim for payment'.[99]

'My Business was the most trifling & lay amongst the poor,' Crabbe recollected in 1781.[100] Some of those poor dwelt in the workhouse which stood on the right-hand side of the road running into Aldeburgh. Many times Crabbe must have entered the 'humble, unpaved cottage, open

---

[97] Crabbe, *Life*, 1947 (1834), p. 29.
[98] Ibid.
[99] Ibid, p. 30.
[100] Letter to Edmund Burke, 26 June 1781. See Crabbe, *Letters*, 1985, p. 11.

to all the winds of heaven, which then did duty for a poor-house, and which can still be seen, standing alone in the middle of a field, facing the railway station'.[101] Huchon wrote this in 1907 when the building still existed – close to where the present-day library, an angular 1960s design, now stands. The grim, desolate lodging place undoubtedly influenced Crabbe's views on deprivation: 'how many poor wretches must he have heard groaning on the seven miserable beds for which five pairs of sheets, four pairs of blankets, and one pair of curtains had to suffice'.[102]

This work in Aldeburgh brought Crabbe almost no income, and it amounted – he later remarked – to 'three years spent in the Misery of a Successless Struggle'.[103] Things looked up for a short while in the summer of 1778 when the Warwickshire militia were quartered in town and his earnings improved, as did his social life – he got on well with the itinerant officers. But that happier time was short lived, and slowly Crabbe fell into abject poverty not dissimilar to that of his patients: 'very often he had not even bread to give his sister Mary, who had come to live with him in his hut'.[104]

An additional burden was the need to conceal these deprivations from his father, who himself was not well off. In his letter of 1781, Crabbe confessed: 'we were unwilling to add to my Father's distress by letting him see ours, and we fasted with much fortitude. Every one knew me to be poor; I was dunned for the most trifling Sums'.[105]

It was at this professional and personal nadir, towards the end of 1779, that Crabbe came to be gazing at the Leech Pond and made up his mind to embark on a different course. A prayer he composed a week later, on 31 December, reveals his feelings – as well as his developing Christian faith:

> A thousand years, most adored Creator, are in thy sight, as one day. So contract, in my sight, my calamities!
>
> The year of sorrow and care, of poverty and disgrace, of disappointment and wrong, is now passing on to join the Eternal. Now, O Lord! Let, I beseech thee, my afflictions and prayers be remembered - let my faults and follies be forgotten!

[101.] Huchon, 1907, p. 64.
[102.] Ibid.
[103.] Letter to Edmund Burke, 26 June 1781. See Crabbe, *Letters,* 1985, p. 12.
[104.] Ibid, p. 69.
[105.] Letter to Edmund Burke, 26 June 1781. See Crabbe, *Letters,* 1985, p. 11.

> The year past, O my God! Let it not be to me a torment - the year coming, if it is Thy will, be it never such.[106]

Unsurprisingly, Crabbe's father was unhappy with this turn of events. In supporting George during two apprenticeships, the old man had spent out to 'afford him an opening into a walk of life higher than their own'.[107] Crabbe's answer was that the apprenticeships had ill prepared him for this calling; a point his father could not really dispute. As Crabbe wryly observed of his Woodbridge apprenticeship, his surgeon master, John Page, was 'a man much esteemed in his profession and I believe he knows something of it, but I had not the good fortune to find it communicated to me'.[108]

How, though, was the budding poet to survive? He wrote to Dudley Long (later Dudley North) – an eminent philanthropist, and brother of Charles Long, the Whig candidate for Aldeburgh – requesting a loan of a small sum. At that time both Dudley and his older brother lived in Saxmundham. Long advanced Crabbe five pounds. And so –

> after settling his affairs at Aldborough, and embarking himself and his whole world substance on board a sloop [the Unity] at Slaughden, to seek his fortune in the Great City, he found himself master of a box of clothes, a small case of surgical instruments, and three pounds in money. During the voyage he lived with the sailors of the vessel, and partook of their fare.[109]

It was a momentous step. Crabbe had decided to abandon the profession from which he felt increasingly disenchanted.

> With the best verses he could write, and with very little more, he quitted the place of his birth; not without the most serious apprehensions of the consequence of such a step – apprehensions which were conquered, and barely conquered, by the more certain evil of the prospect before him, should he remain where he was.[110]

[106.] Crabbe, *Life*, 1947 (1834), pp. 37–38.
[107.] Ibid, p. 39.
[108.] Letter to Edmund Burke, 26 June 1781. See Crabbe, *Letters*, 1985, p. 10.
[109.] Crabbe, *Life*, 1947 (1834), p. 39.
[110.] Ibid, p. 38.

Chapter 2

Growing to Manhood

Love, London and Literary Success

Parham: A young lady that would just suit you

The hour arrived! I sigh'd and said,
How soon the happiest hours are fled!
On wings of down they lately flew,
But then their moments pass'd with you;
And still with you could I but be,
On downy wings they'd always flee.
Say, did you not, the way you went,
Feel the soft balm of gay content?
Say, did you not all pleasures find,
Of which you left so few behind?
I think you did: for well I know
My parting prayer would make it so![1]

Crabbe's decision at the Leech Pond marked not only the abandonment of his profession. He was also leaving the woman with whom he had fallen in love.

---

[1]. 'A Farewell', 1779. See Crabbe, *Poetical Works*, 1932, p. 9.

He had met Sarah Elmy during his time in Woodbridge, while apprenticed to John Page. A group of young men including Crabbe would meet at the pub in the evenings, where they would have animated discussions and "converse on the subjects which they were severally studying" over a frugal supper.[2]

But naturally scholarship was not the only topic of discourse. One of Crabbe's drinking companions was another aspiring surgeon, William Springall Levett, himself the son of an Aldeburgh surgeon – the same friend who would later upbraid Crabbe for having fallen back into manual labour at Slaughden Quay. Levett was wooing a young woman of Framlingham whose great friend and companion was Sarah Elmy, then living in the neighbouring village of Parham. One day Levett made a proposal: 'Why, George, you shall go with me to Parham: there is a young lady there that would just suit you.'[3]

Parham is a sleepy village some twelve miles west of Aldeburgh. It is embedded in rural, green Suffolk – in stark contrast to the coastal landscape where Crabbe grew up. Its flint parish church, St Mary the Virgin, has a square tower built by William de Ufford, Earl of Suffolk, in the fourteenth century. Even today, its population totals just some three hundred.

The village came to be as pivotal in Crabbe's personal relationships as Aldeburgh would be in his writings. In 1772, Crabbe and Levett spent a day there with the two young women, an occasion that – it turned out – 'decided his matrimonial lot in life'.[4] In the words of the critic and cleric John Mitford, in a review of 1834 for *The Gentleman's Magazine*, Crabbe 'accordingly went, was introduced, made himself agreeable, put as much *sugar on his cake* as he could, spent a day in the society of the fair one, [and] fell in love' (Mitford notes that the expression in italics reflected Crabbe's behaviour towards the female sex).[5]

Sarah was staying at that time with her uncle, John Tovell, a wealthy yeoman, and Crabbe's subsequent visits to the house gave him an insight into a way of life very different from his own. The experience perhaps raised his sights – not least towards prospects in London.

---

[2] Crabbe, *Life*, 1947 (1834), p. 18.

[3] Ibid, p. 19.

[4] Ibid, p. 19.

[5] John Mitford, 'Life of the Poet Crabbe', *The Gentleman's Magazine*, new series, Vol. 1, March 1834: p. 257. Mitford has embellished the account given in the son's biography, although whether through hearsay or his own imaginative speculation is unclear.

According to Crabbe's son, Sarah was 'remarkably pretty; she had a lively disposition'.[6] She was moreover an intellectual match; as the couple's son, George, observed in retrospect: 'she possessed naturally a great share of penetration and acuteness, a firm, unflinching spirit, and very warm and feeling heart'.[7]

If their acquaintance offered Crabbe a vision of higher society – higher than that he had known – Parham was, for Sarah, something of a step down. Accustomed to the genteel society of Beccles, the market town where she had grown up, she was out of place in the village. Parham was isolated, a place which the 'refinements of modern civilisation had hardly penetrated', with the result that the village and other nearby districts were 'vegetating in the dullness of their sluggish life'.[8] The yeomen, one step higher than the farmers, remained rooted to the soil: John Tovell belonged to a family that had been established in the village for more than two hundred years.

And yet, compared with his sister – Sarah's widowed mother – Tovell was comfortably off. He would help with expenses, and invited Sarah, the oldest of the three girls, to make long stays with his family at Ducking Hall, a moated dwelling in Parham.

At first, Crabbe was barely tolerated. No doubt protective of Sarah, Tovell was also of 'a class ever jealous of the privileges of literature'. 'What good does their d——d learning do them?', he would say, in a swipe at the erudition Crabbe had acquired.[9] In time, though, Crabbe endeared himself – even if he still had to put up with occasional sneers about his 'd——d learning'. However humble his position may have been, his innate intelligence marked him out from the men of Parham, giving him 'a superiority over these rustics of which Sarah Elmy speedily became aware'.[10]

Before long, Crabbe found himself immersed in Tovell family life at Ducking Hall. His vivid extended description of dinner in 'The Widow's Tale' (*Tales*, 1812) is thought to draw on their family meals – with the servants sitting at a side table. Crabbe and 'Mira' (his name for Sarah) may well have had similar thoughts about the rustic food being served, to those of his character Nancy Moss:

[6.] Crabbe, *Life*, 1947 (1834), p. 33.
[7.] Ibid, p. 182.
[8.] Huchon, 1907, p. 48.
[9.] Crabbe, *Life*, 1947 (1834), p. 32.
[10.] Huchon, 1907, p. 52.

Used to spare meals, disposed in manner pure,
Her father's kitchen she could ill endure;
Where by the steaming beef he hungry sat,
And laid at once a pound upon his plate;
Hot from the field, her eager brother seized
An equal part, and hunger's rage appeased;
The air, surcharged with moisture, flagg'd around,
And the offended damsel sigh'd and frown'd;
The swelling fat in lumps conglomerate laid,
And fancy's sickness seized the loathing maid:
But when the men beside their station took,
The maidens with them, and with these the cook;
When one huge wooden bowl before them stood,
Fill'd with huge balls of farinaceous food;
With bacon, mass saline, where never lean
Beneath the brown and bristly rind was seen;
When from a single horn the party drew
Their copious droughts of heavy ale and new;
When the coarse cloth she saw, with many a stain,
Soil'd by rude hinds who cut and came again –
She could not breathe; but, with a heavy sigh,
Rein'd the fair neck, and shut th' offended eye;
She minced the sanguine flesh in frustums fine,
And wonder'd much to see the creatures dine:[11]

The food may have been fatty and unrefined, but Crabbe's outings to Parham marked a time of burgeoning romance. In *Tales of the Hall* (1819), he writes – in the voice of the character Richard, who is entranced by Matilda, the rector's daughter – about this time in his life. The lines possess a lyricism that is at odds with the grit of his poems drawing on Aldeburgh:

O! days remember'd well! remember'd all!
The bitter-sweet, the honey, and the gall;
Those garden rambles in the silent night,
Those trees so shady, and that moon so bright;
That thick-set alley by the arbour closed,
That woodbine seat where we at last reposed;
And then the hopes that came and then were gone,

[11.] 'The Widow's Tale', Tale VII, *Tales*. See Crabbe, *Poetical Works,* 1932, p. 256.

> *Quick as the clouds beneath the moon past on:*
> *Now, in this instant, shall my love be shown,*
> *I said—O! no, the happy time is flown!*[12]

Ducking Hall, site of those garden rambles and trysts on the woodbine seat, is no more. This was the house that Crabbe, through Sarah, ultimately came to own, after Tovell died in 1792. By the 1830s, the house had been altered and modernised, becoming known as Parham Lodge: the moat was filled in and rooms added. Then it was entirely rebuilt in 1851–52 – the east wing of the present house is thought to be where Ducking Hall originally stood.

There is an illustration in the third volume of the 1834 edition of Crabbe's works, a reproduction of a watercolour drawing by Clarkson Stanfield. It is now in the Victoria and Albert Museum and entitled *Old Parham Hall, Suffolk, the Moathouse of the Poet Crabbe*. This two-storied house, with gables and chimneys, its upper floor projecting slightly over the lower, still exists: it is on the crest of the hill of Parham, a little beyond the church, ascending from the valley towards Little Parham. But despite the watercolour's title, this house – Old Parham Hall – was not Crabbe's, although it is so picturesque, as Huchon observes, that 'one would wish that the poet had inhabited it'.[13]

John Mitford – who was vicar of Benhall from 1810 and 'a lover of gossip and small details', in Huchon's words – asserted as much at the time: 'The vignette of his house at Parham is not correct. That was not his house which lies at the top of the hill.'[14] The house where Mr Crabbe resided at Parham, as Mitford confirmed in a review of 1834, 'is very near the seat of Mr Dudley North'.[15] (North, who changed his name from Dudley Long upon inheriting the estate of Little Glemham in 1789, became a close friend of Crabbe's.)

The pursuit of Sarah Elmy led Crabbe to the rich vegetation of inland Suffolk including the town of Beccles, where she would visit her mother. Her father, a tanner there, had failed in his business and gone to make a new life for himself in Guadeloupe, where he had died some time

---

[12.] 'Adventures of Richard Concluded', Book VI, *Tales of the Hall*. See Crabbe, *Poetical Works*, 1932, p. 367.
[13.] Huchon, 1907, p. 49. The assertion can be found within one of Mitford's 'almost illegible' notes, now in the British Museum.
[14.] Ibid, n. 4.
[15.] Mitford, 1834, p. 259.

Figure 9. Not Crabbe's house: Parham Hall, Suffolk: Drawing by Clarkson Stanfield, engraved by E. Finden for The Poetical Works of the Rev. George Crabbe (London: John Murray, 1834)

before. In Beccles, where Sarah's educated family counted themselves among the local gentry, Crabbe found 'a society more adapted to his requirements'.[16]

Crabbe would spend much time walking the twenty-four miles from Aldeburgh to see her in Beccles – a welcome escape from his failing attempts to establish a medical practice in the coastal town. It was on these walks that he passed through the scenery that he would evoke in the first part of 'The Lover's Journey' (*Tales*, 1812). This recounts how a young man, Orlando, travels to meet his sweetheart, Laura: first he journeys over the 'barren heath beside the coast' where the 'neat low gorse […] with golden bloom, / Delights each sense, is beauty, is perfume'.

[16.] Crabbe, *Life*, 1947 (1834), p. 32.

Growing to Manhood

Then he heads inland, where:

The very lane has sweets that all admire,
The rambling suckling and the vigorous briar;
See! wholesome wormwood grows beside the way,
Where, dew-pressed yet, the dog-rose bends the spray;
Fresh herbs the fields, fair shrubs the banks adorn,
And snow-white bloom falls flaky from the thorn;

When on arrival Orlando discovers his love has gone to visit a friend, he is consumed with jealousy and anger and his view of his natural surroundings changes accordingly:

I hate these long green lanes; there's nothing seen
In this vile country but eternal green;
Woods! waters! meadows! will they never end?
'Tis a vile prospect: – Gone to see a friend! –[17]

Crabbe's son speculates that Orlando's disappointment reflects Crabbe's own, when – on one of his romantic visits – he discovered that Sarah had gone out to see a friend.[18] A similar self-torment is described in *Tales of the Hall*, in which the narrator, Richard, finds his beloved, Matilda, in the company of a rival suitor:

But when I enter'd that pernicious room,
Gloomy it look'd, and painful was the gloom;
And jealous was the pain, and deep the sigh
Caused by this gloom, and pain, and jealousy,
For there Matilda sat, and her beside
That rival soldier, with a soldier's pride;[19]

---

[17] 'The Lover's Journey', Tale X, *Tales*, 54–59, 260–63. See Crabbe, *Poems*, 2015, p. 232, p. 238.
[18] Crabbe, *Life*, 1947 (1834), p. 33.
[19] 'Adventures of Richard Concluded', Book VI, *Tales of the Hall*. See Crabbe, *Poetical Works*, 1932, p. 368. On Richard's turbulent and changing feelings towards Matilda, see Frank S. Whitehead, *George Crabbe: A Reappraisal* (Selinsgrove: Susquehanna University Press, 1995), pp. 151–52.

In reality, Crabbe's relationship was going well. His parents, approving of their son's choice, invited Sarah to stay at Aldeburgh, where she was well received and made good friends with Crabbe's sister, Mary. It was during one of these visits, however, that Crabbe fell ill with a dangerous fever and for a time could not walk upright. He recorded the joy and relief of his convalescence, in returning to his best-loved occupations of searching 'for fuci [olive-brown seaweed] on the shore, or to botanise on the heath':[20]

> *See! one relieved from anguish, and to-day*
> *Allow'd to walk, and look an hour away;*
> *Two months confined by fever, frenzy, pain,*
> *He comes abroad, and is himself again:*
> *'Twas in the spring, when carried to the place,*
> *The snow fell down and melted in his face.*
> *'Tis summer now; all objects gay and new,*
> *Smiling alike the viewer and the view:*
> *He stops as one unwilling to advance,*
> *Without another and another glance;*
> *With what a pure and simple joy he sees*
> *Those sheep and cattle browzing at their ease;*
> *Easy himself, there's nothing breathes or moves*
> *But he would cherish – all that lives he loves:*[21]

With Crabbe's illness, Sarah returned to Parham – but then herself succumbed to a similar fever that was yet 'more violent and alarming' – so severe that her recovery was not expected. Crabbe was invited to be with her. His son writes: 'I remember being greatly affected, at a very early period, by hearing him describe the feelings with which he went into a small garden her uncle had given her, to water her flowers; intending, after her death, to take them to Aldborough, and keep them for ever.'[22]

Sarah recovered. But then tragedy struck elsewhere: the Tovells lost their only child, a girl of fourteen, in what Crabbe's son describes as 'a calamity of the severest kind'. She was 'cut off in a few days by an inflammatory sore throat. Her parents were bowed down to the earth;

---

[20] Crabbe, *Life*, 1947 (1834), p. 34.
[21] 'The Hospital and Governors', Letter XVII, *The Borough*. See Crabbe, *Poetical Works*, 1932, p. 174.
[22] Crabbe, *Life*, 1947 (1834), p. 35.

so sudden and unexpected was the blow. It made a permanent alteration at Parham. Mr Tovell's health declined from that period, though he lived many years with a broken spirit.'[23]

Crabbe's spirits were buoyed by the requited affection from Sarah, but she was not keen to marry where there were no clear prospects of a livelihood. He 'deliberated often and long – "resolved and re-resolved" – and again doubted', but finally made up his mind 'to go to London and venture all'.[24] Upon departing, he wrote lines of wistful farewell to Sarah: 'The hour arrived! I sigh'd and said, / How soon the happiest hours are fled'. But their relationship continued. She became his fiancée and their engagement was to last for eight years before Crabbe felt finally in a position to marry.

Parham, romance and Sarah Elmy, the lanes and byways of inland Suffolk – these coinciding experiences and settings had changed Crabbe's perspective and determined his future. The wild coastal landscape of Aldeburgh had been tempered by the softer side of the county.

Above all, by the early 1780s, he had achieved a glimpse of London – and with it, kindled the dream of patronage. He allowed himself to bask in thoughts of future success – as later expressed in his poem 'The Patron' (*Tales*):

> 'A little time, and he should burst to light,
> And admiration of the world excite;
> And every friend, now cool, and apt to blame
> His fond pursuit, would wonder at his fame.'
> When led by fancy, and from view retired,
> He called before him all his heart desired;
> 'Fame shall be mine – then wealth shall I possess,
> And beauty next an ardent lover bless;'[25]

Had his relationship with Sarah played a part in this decision to 'venture all' on a new path? His son speculates: 'Whether my father's more frequent visits to Parham, growing dislike to his profession, or increasing attachment to poetical composition, contributed most to his ultimate abandonment of medicine, I do not profess to tell.'[26]

[23.] Ibid.
[24.] Ibid, p. 37.
[25.] 'The Patron', Tale V, *Tales*, 63–70. See Crabbe, *Selected Poems*, 2015, p. 157.
[26.] Crabbe, *Life*, 1947 (1834), p. 36.

London: I have parted with my money, sold my wardrobe

Crabbe had never heard of Thomas Chatterton. The fate of that young poet, later a subject of fascination to the Romantics – and depicted in a painting of 1856 by the pre-Raphaelite Henry Wallis – might have deterred him from abandoning the medical profession and trying his luck as a writer. The talented Chatterton, memorialised by William Wordsworth as 'the marvellous Boy, / The sleepless Soul that perished in his pride,' had come to London as an adolescent and attempted, without success, to find outlets for his compositions. Crushed by his inability to achieve recognition, he committed suicide at the age of seventeen.

That was in 1770, a decade before Crabbe arrived in the capital. At that moment, the times seemed fortuitous for an aspiring poet. 'The field may be said to have laid open before him', Crabbe's son remarks. Alexander Pope and Jonathan Swift, literary giants of the eighteenth century, had long since passed away (in 1744 and 1745 respectively), and the style of each – although still dominant – had for so long been imitated and traduced that 'the world was not unlikely to welcome someone who should strike into a newer path'.[27]

The satirist Charles Churchill, the classical scholar and poet Thomas Gray, and the 'inimitable' Oliver Goldsmith had also all gone, and the 'stupendous [Samuel] Johnson, unrivalled in general literature, had from an early period, withdrawn himself from poetry'. (Johnson died in 1784. As a man of letters, however, he remained active and prolific into old age). William Cowper had not yet appeared on the scene, and Robert Burns was as yet unknown beyond his obscure circle of Ayrshire villagers.

The literary landscape, then, gave Crabbe cause for optimism. If he had foreseen the difficulties and disappointments to come, he might have stayed in Aldeburgh – or at the very least, come to London and 'engaged himself to beat the mortar in some dispensary'. But he was ambitious and optimistic, and hopes prevailed over fears: 'his mind soared and exulted when he suddenly felt himself freed from the drudgery and anxieties of his hated profession'.[28]

After his arrival by river in early 1780, Crabbe took lodgings in the City, so as to be close to his only acquaintance in London, a Mrs Burcham, who had been a friend of Sarah Elmy and was the wife of a linen draper

---

[27] Crabbe, *Life*, 1947 (1834), p. 42.
[28] Ibid, p. 43.

in Cornhill. His lodgings were close to the Exchange, in the house of a hairdresser, Mr Vickery ('rather too expensive', as he complained to Sarah, 'but very convenient').[29] Some months later, the Vickerys moved house and Crabbe went with them to Bishopsgate Street.

In his early days in London, Crabbe spent the evenings at a small coffee house near the Exchange. Here, he conversed with other young men, 'most of them teachers of mathematics', and many of them just as obscure as himself, but rising later to prominence and distinction of one kind or another. He wandered the city by day and night, notwithstanding a strange fear ('for reasons which he might not himself be able to assign') of 'going to the west end of the town', and in June he witnessed the Gordon Riots, during which Newgate Prison was stormed and burned.[30] Sometimes he would walk out to the countryside 'with a small edition of Ovid, or Horace, or Catullus, in his pocket'. In later life, he described those little volumes as the 'companions of his adversity'.[31]

Classical poetry provided only transient escape. His urgent and hardest task was to find a patron. He wrote letters to several potential benefactors, all the while penning short passages of verse which he sent to various publishers. Before long, his financial situation was dire. He wrote regularly to Sarah Elmy (Mira), by then his fiancée, assembling his letters in a 'Poet's Journal' begun in April 1780 – a bleak record of three months of ebbing hope. On 21 April, the date of his first entry, his mood was still one of brave optimism:

> I DEDICATE to you, my dear Mira, this Journal, and I hope it will be some amusement. God only knows what is to be my lot; but I have, as far as I can, taken your old advice, and turned affliction's better part outward and am determined to reap as much consolation from my prospects as possible; so that, whatever befalls me, I will endeavour to suppose it has its benefits, though I cannot immediately see them.[32]

[29.] 'The Poet's Journal', 21 April 1780, quoted in Crabbe, *Life*, 1947 (1834), p. 50.

[30.] Crabbe, 1816, p. 513. 'The Poet's Journal', 8 June 1780, quoted in Crabbe, *Life*, 1947 (1834), pp. 71–74.

[31.] Crabbe, *Life*, 1947 (1834), p. 46.

[32.] 'The Poet's Journal', 21 April 1780, quoted in Crabbe, *Life*, 1947 (1834), pp. 49–50.

In a matter of days, and with his work being roundly rejected, he was forced to pawn what few articles he had:

> I don't think there's a man in London worth but fourpence-halfpenny – for I've this very moment sent seven farthings for a pint of porter – who is so resigned to his poverty.[33]

> O! my dear Mira, how you distress me: you inquire into my affairs, and love not to be denied – yet you must. To what purpose should I tell you the particulars of my gloomy situation; that I have parted with my money, sold my *wardrobe*, pawned my watch, am in debt to my landlord, and finally, at some loss how to eat a week longer?[34]

Tempted into buying three volumes of the works of John Dryden, which he bid down from five shillings to three shillings and sixpence, he found himself with almost nothing:

> It's the vilest thing in the world to have but one coat. My only one has happened with a mischance, and how to manage it is some difficulty. A confounded stove's modish ornament caught its elbow, and rent it halfway. Pinioned to the side it came home, and I ran deploring to my loft. In the dilemma, it occurred to me to turn tailor myself; but how to get materials to work with puzzled me. At last I went running down in a hurry, with three or four sheets of paper in my hand, and begged for a needle &c., to sew them together. This finished my job, and but that it is somewhat thicker, the elbow is a good one yet.

> These are foolish things, Mira, to write or speak, and we may laugh at them; but I'll be bound to say they are much more likely to make a man cry, where they *happen* – though I was too much of a philosopher for *that*, however, not one of those who preferred a ragged coat to a whole one.[35]

[33.] 'The Poet's Journal', 10 May 1780. Ibid, p. 56.
[34.] 'The Poet's Journal', 12 May 1780. Ibid, p. 57.
[35.] 'The Poet's Journal', 20 May 1780. Ibid, pp. 58–59.

Crabbe persisted in his hunt for a benefactor with the same philosophic tenacity. He applied to Lord Frederick North (then Prime Minister) for employment 'in any Department that I should be thought qualified for', to Lord Shelburne (who was to become Home Secretary in 1782, and later briefly Prime Minister), and to the Lord Chancellor of the day, Lord Thurlow.[36]

In his letter to Shelburne (relayed for Sarah's benefit in 'The Poet's Journal'), he summarised his predicament in words that were equally damning of his professional failures and his Suffolk origins, while reserving harsh censure for the Prime Minister:

> Your Lordship will pardon me the relation of a late and unsuccessful attempt to become useful to myself and the community I live in. Starving as an apothecary, in a little venal borough in Suffolk, it was there suggested to me that Lord North, the present minister, was a man of that liberal disposition, that I might hope success from a representation of my particular circumstances to him. [...] at length a lingering refusal, brought me by an insolent domestic, determined my suit, and my opinion of his Lordship's private virtues.[37]

It was a time of constant disappointment and acute worry. Despite the misgivings Crabbe expressed in his letter to Shelburne, the life of an apothecary began – once more – to present a stolid and stable alternative to his creative ambitions. 'His circumstances were now, indeed, fearfully critical: absolute want stared him in the face: a gaol seemed the only immediate refuge for his head; and the best he could hope for was, dismissing all his dreams of literary distinction, to find the means of daily bread in the capacity of a druggist's assistant.'[38]

[36.] Letter to Edmund Burke, 26 June 1781. See Crabbe, *Letters,* 1985, p. 12. Crabbe was admitted to Lord North, 'and treated with more attention that I should expect, though with none of that Affability I had been led to hope for'. Ultimately, though, the endeavour was futile: Crabbe persisted in vain – over several months – to gain a firm answer to his petition, before finally being dismissed 'with some Severity'.

[37.] 'The Poet's Journal', 6 June 1780, quoted in Crabbe, *Life,* 1947 (1834), p. 68.

[38.] Crabbe, *Life,* 1947 (1834), p. 78.

London: The hand that rescued him

Then came a life-changing event. Crabbe made one final, desperate effort at obtaining funds and 'he fixed, impelled by some propitious influence, in some happy moment, upon EDMUND BURKE – one of the first of Englishmen, and, in the capacity and energy of his mind, one of the greatest of human beings.'[39] Towards the end of February or the beginning of March 1781, he wrote to Burke, setting out his destitution in the plain terms of a man with nothing to lose: 'I am one of those outcasts on the world who are without a friend, without employment, and without bread.' He added:

> I had a partial Father, who gave me a better Education than his broken Fortune wou'd have allowed & a better than was necessary as he could give me that only. I was design'd for the Profession of Physic, but not having sufficient to complete the requisite Studies, the Design but served to convince me of a Parent's Affection, & the Error it occasion'd.[40]

Continuing to lay bare his hardship and to deprecate his talents, he related how, the April before, he had come to London with five pounds and:

> flatter'd myself it was sufficient to supply me with the common Necessaries of Life, til *such of* my Abillities shou'd procure me more ... I knew little of the World & had read Books only; I wrote, and fancied Perfection in my Compositions, when I wanted bread, they promised me Affluence, and sooth'd me with Dreams of Reputation, whilst my Appearance subjected me to Contempt.
>
> Time, Reflection, & Want, have shown me my Mistake[41]

He recounted how he had been deceived by a printer, fallen into debt (owing some fourteen pounds), and was steeling himself to 'prepare for prison'. Forty years later, he would relate how the delivery of the letter

---

[39.] Crabbe, *Life*, 1947 (1834), p. 79.
[40.] Letter to Edmund Burke, February-March 1781. See Crabbe, *Letters*, 1985, p. 3.
[41.] Ibid.

occasioned a 'dark night of the soul': he left Burke's door 'in such a state of agitation that I walked Westminster Bridge backwards and forwards until daylight'.[42]

Crabbe's 'confessional' to Burke ended on a note of abject despair:

> I will call upon You Sir tomorrow & if I have not the Happiness to obtain Credit with You, I will submit to my Fate: My Existence is a Pain to me, & every one near & dear to me are distress'd in my Distresses; [...] I have only to hope for a speedy End to a Life so uncompromisingly begun: In which (tho it ought not to be boasted of) I can reap some Consolation from looking to the End of it.[43]

Burke (1729–1897) was already an influential Whig statesman, 'engaged in the hottest turmoils of parliamentary opposition'. The second son of a Dublin attorney, he had been educated at Baltimore School, County Kildare, and Trinity College, Dublin. He was a Member of Parliament for nearly thirty years, from 1765 to 1794, and served as Paymaster of the Forces in the 1782 government of the liberal Lord Rockingham, and in the Fox-North coalition of the following year.

At the time of Crabbe's approach, Burke was a leading liberal voice who would go on to champion numerous progressive causes, denouncing the persecution of Catholics in Ireland; backing the American colonies over their grievances; supporting American independence and pursuing the impeachment of Warren Hastings, governor general of India, for corruption and abuse of power. Yet he was also to write a political pamphlet ('Reflections on the Revolution in France', November 1790) which became one of the best-known intellectual attacks on the French Revolution – as well as a defining tract of the political philosophy of conservatism. In this, he denounced the revolution as a 'disaster' and the revolutionaries as 'a swinish multitude' under whose 'hoofs' learning would be crushed.

[42.] Crabbe related this in the course of a walk in Scotland in 1822, in the company of Sir Walter Scott and his son-in-law, John Gibson Lockhart. See Lockhart, letter to George Crabbe (the poet's son), 26 December 1833: Crabbe, *Life*, 1947 (1834), p. 246.

[43.] Letter to Edmund Burke, February–March 1781. See Crabbe, *Letters*, 1985, p. 5.

Despite not being particularly affluent himself, Burke gave Crabbe's letter and the enclosed verses his serious attention. The poet's son recounts:

> He immediately appointed an hour for my father to call upon him at his house in London; and the short interview that ensued, entirely, and for ever, changed the nature of his worldly fortunes. He was, in the common phrase, 'a made man.'[44]

Burke's intervention was critical. His son continues: 'Mr Crabbe had afterwards many other friends, kind, liberal and powerful, who assisted him in his professional career; but, it was one hand alone that rescued him when he was *sinking*.' Yet as the younger Crabbe also aptly remarks, had not his father's writings 'possessed the marks of real genius, the applicant would probably have been dismissed with a little pecuniary assistance'.[45] Burke proffered not only financial support but literary advice, identifying *The Library* and *The Village* as 'two poems of a somewhat superior kind'.[46] The former was selected for swift publication – a philosophical exposition on the value of books as consolation and balm to a person in distress, but with the caution that they can in turn mislead or cause pain.

> *But what strange art, what magic can dispose*
> *The troubled mind to change its native woes?*
> *Or lead us willing from ourselves, to see*
> *Others more wretched, more undone than we?*
> *This books can do; – nor this alone; they give*
> *New views to life, and teach us how to live;*
> *They soothe the grieved, the stubborn they chastise,*
> *Fools they admonish, and confirm the wise:*
> *Their aid they yield to all: they never shun*
> *The man of sorrow, nor the wretch undone:*
> *Unlike the hard, the selfish, and the proud,*
> *They fly not sullen from the suppliant crowd;*
> *Nor tell to various people various things,*
> *But show to subjects, what they show to kings.*[47]

[44.] Crabbe, *Life*, 1947 (1834), p. 82.
[45.] Ibid, pp. 82–83.
[46.] Crabbe, 1816, p. 514.
[47.] *The Library.* See Crabbe, *Poetical Works,* 1932, pp. 25–26.

Burke encouraged Crabbe to make revisions and add finishing touches to *The Library*. Two months elapsed, and during some of this time Crabbe was living again with the Elmys in Beccles – and adding names to the list of potential subscribers for his poem in anticipation of its publication. His break for freedom in London, so nearly a disaster, had paid off – if only just.

In Beccles between April and June, Crabbe was taking stock of the painful experiences he had gone through on the journey to patronage and literary attainment. Back in London in June 1781, he wrote to Burke, giving what he called a 'farther Account of myself'. The letter is the fullest description of his life to date, including what he saw as the 'unlucky Opportunity that had afforded itself at Aldborough' – namely the chance to take on the apothecary business – and how, 'after three years spent in the Misery of a Successless Struggle, I found it necessary for me to depart and I came to London'.[48]

Meanwhile Burke took *The Library* to a publisher who agreed to issue it for two hundred subscribers. The poem appeared on 24 July, under the imprint of the well-known London bookseller James Dodsley, whose shop was in Pall Mall. The success of the poem led two years later to the publication of *The Village*.

Burke had provided monetary support and help in publishing Crabbe's writings. But he also became an enthusiastic friend and mentor. As Crabbe's son describes, Burke warmed instinctively to the younger man:

> Had there appeared any offensive peculiarities of manner and address – either presumption or meanness – though the young poet might have received both kindness and patronage, can anyone dream that Mr. Burke would have at once taken up his cause with the zeal of a friend, domesticated him under his own roof, and treated him like a son? In mentioning his new *protégé* a few days afterwards, to Reynolds [Sir Joshua Reynolds, the painter], Burke said, "He has the mind and feelings of a gentleman."[49]

In July, Crabbe was also invited to Burke's house, Gregories, in the latter's constituency in the market town of Beaconsfield, some twenty miles west of London. Here, he

---

[48.] Letter to Edmund Burke, 26 June 1781. See Crabbe, *Letters*, 1985, pp. 9–12.
[49.] Crabbe, *Life*, 1947 (1834), p. 83.

> was encouraged to lay open his views, past and present; to display whatever reading and acquirements he possessed, to explain the causes of his disappointments, and the cloudiness of his prospects; in short, he concealed nothing from a friend so able to guide inexperience, and so willing to pardon inadvertence.[50]

It was a watershed for the young poet; and in his biography of his father, Crabbe's son expresses enduring gratitude to Burke for his kindness and the turn of events that his patronage marked:

> This obscure young writer could contribute in nothing to the reputation of a statesman and orator, at the very apex of influence and renown; yet never had he been so affectionately received as when, a penniless dependant, he first entered the hall of that beautiful mansion[51]

Moreover, Crabbe was given an entrée to influential circles. Through Burke and 'under this happy roof' he met various eminences of London society, including Sir Joshua Reynolds and the Whig politician Charles James Fox. Through the clubs at which Burke was a member, he also came into contact with Dr Samuel Johnson, who read and revised the poem subsequently published as *The Village*. One maxim of Johnson's had a lasting impression: 'Never fear putting the strongest and best things you can think of into the mouth of your speaker, whatever may be his condition.'[52]

But Burke's patronage also brought with it a second crucial development. On a walk together at Beaconsfield, he drew from Crabbe that the poet felt a 'strong partiality' for the church. This was already becoming evident during his time in London, where on one occasion he enjoyed a sermon 'by my favourite clergyman, at St Dunstan's' (this was the Rev. Thomas Winstanley, of Trinity College, Cambridge), 'a man who seems as if already half way to Heaven', and sent the text of the entire sermon, written out by memory, to Sarah Elmy.[53]

His faith, too, supported him during some of these times, as is clear from his 'Poet's Journal' of letters to Sarah, and he sought guidance through prayer. On 22 May 1780, the day after he praised Winstanley's

---

[50] Crabbe, 1816, p. 514.
[51] Crabbe, *Life*, 1947 (1834), p. 87.
[52] Ibid, pp. 88–89.
[53] 'The Poet's Journal', 21 May 1780, quoted in Crabbe, *Life*, 1947 (1834), pp. 60–63.

sermon, and not quite a year before he secured the life-changing patronage of Burke, he had prayed for the success of his 'Poetic Epistles' – a book of some 450 lines on which he was then engaged: 'I have just now finished my book, and, if I may so say, consecrated it, by begging of Him, who alone can direct all things, to give me success in it, or patience under any disappointment I may meet with from its wanting that.'[54]

Burke saw that in Crabbe's godliness lay a possible future path. 'It is most fortunate,' he remarked, 'that your father exerted himself to send you to that second school; without a little Latin we should have made nothing of you: now, I think we shall succeed.'[55]

More enthusiastically, the politician told Sir Joshua Reynolds that Mr Crabbe 'appears to know something of everything'. As Crabbe's son surmises: 'Burke himself was a strong advocate for storing the mind with multiform knowledge, rather than confining it to one narrow line of study, and he often remarked, that there was no profession in which diversity of information was more useful, and, indeed necessary, than that of a clergyman.'[56]

There was one major obstacle, however. Despite his 'little Latin' and multifarious knowledge, Crabbe did not have the university degree that would qualify him for holy orders. Undeterred, Burke nonetheless set about trying to procure the obtaining of holy orders via the Bishop of Norwich, Dr Philip Yonge (of whom the diarist Sylas Neville noted, with an acerbity worthy of Crabbe himself: 'This fat blown-up fellow is said to be one of the best preachers in the Establishment. But it is low in preachers, if that is the case.')[57] And thanks to the favourable representations of Dudley and Charles Long, the brothers in Saxmundham who had become supporters, Crabbe was eventually successful.

He passed 'a very creditable examination' and was duly admitted to deacon's orders in London on 21 December 1781 by the Bishop of Norwich – and licensed as a curate to the Rev. James Benet, rector of Aldeburgh.[58] The Bishop ordained him priest in August the following year in Norwich Cathedral. The location of the curacy was a source of some dismay, however; on learning of it, Crabbe had written to Burke: 'It happens a little unfortunately that the Place my friends [Dudley

---

[54.] 'The Poet's Journal', 22 May 1780, quoted in Crabbe, *Life*, 1947 (1834), p. 64.
[55.] Crabbe, *Life*, 1947 (1834), p. 86.
[56.] Crabbe, *Life*, 1947 (1834), p. 86.
[57.] Sylas Neville, *Diary, 1767–1788*, edited by Basil Cozens-Hardy (London: Oxford University Press, 1950), p. 175.
[58.] Crabbe, *Life*, 1947 (1834), p. 90.

and Charles Long] here, chose for me is Aldbro' and in this Interval of Suspense I consider it, more than a little so [...] I cannot say to them that I was very miserable & miserably treated & *cannot* esteem a great part of the Inhabitants who must be [con]scious that they did not use me well".[59]

And so, with some misgivings, Crabbe was to return to Aldeburgh to start a new chapter in the 'little venal borough' of former days.

Aldeburgh revisited:
A prophet is not without honour...

London had been the catalyst of Crabbe's new life. But in only a short time, he was back where he had begun, in Aldeburgh. Now, though, his fortunes had transformed since that moment of reckoning when he stood at the Leech Pond. As his son comments, 'he must have been more than man had he not exulted at the change'.[60]

Crabbe's reputation on leaving the town had been low. He had failed at all he had tried, and was not remembered with any great respect or affection by the townsfolk:

> He left his home a deserter from his profession, with the imputation of having failed in it from wanting even common abilities for the discharge of its duties – in the estimation of the ruder natives, who had witnessed his manual awkwardness in the seafaring pursuits of the place, 'a lubber', and 'a fool', perhaps considered even by those who recognised something of his literary talent, as a harebrained visionary, never designed to settle to anything with steadiness and sober resolution; on all hands convicted certainly of the 'crime of poverty', and dismissed from view as a destitute and hopeless outcast.[61]

By the time of his return, which was probably soon after his ordination in December 1781, the 'harebrained visionary' had not only found a patron in the form of Edmund Burke, but had enjoyed some initial success with his writing (*The Library*, 1781), met with literary luminaries such as Samuel Johnson, and been ordained a deacon, enabling him to be appointed to the curacy at Aldeburgh. 'He returned, a man of

---

[59.] Letter to Edmund Burke, 9 October 1781. See Crabbe, *Letters*, 1985, p. 21.
[60.] Crabbe, *Life*, 1947 (1834), p. 91.
[61.] Ibid.

acknowledged talents; a successful author, patronised and befriended by some of the leading characters in the kingdom; and a clergyman with every prospect of preferment in the church.'[62]

If Crabbe had changed, so too had his family circumstances – for the worse. In his nearly two years away, his mother had died, in July 1780 – succumbing to the 'dropsy', or painful swelling induced by water retention (probably the result of heart failure). The loss of his mother was hard for Crabbe to bear and at every turn he was reminded of her absence. The experience may lie behind his account of sudden bereavement in his later poem, *The Parish Register* (1807), where the 'Wife of Farmer Frankford dies in Prime of Life':

> *Arrived at home, how then they gazed around,*
> *In every place, – where she – no more was found; –*
> *The seat at table she was wont to fill;*
> *The fire-side chair, still set, but vacant still;*
> *The garden-walks, a labour all her own;*
> *The latticed bower, with trailing shrubs o'er-grown;*
> *The Sunday-pew she fill'd with all her race, –*
> *Each place of hers, was now a secret place.*[63]

Meanwhile, Crabbe's 'father's temper and habits were not the better for losing the wholesome restraints of her presence'.[64] Their relationship remained strained: in his letter to Burke in October 1871, Crabbe had admitted:

> My Affection & my Duty to my father, leads me to avoid him. – It is only to you Sir that I can say these things – my Father & I are in perfect Agreement; we parted with every Appearance of it & I am persuaded there was Deceit in none: but if I live in the same Place; I know that it is impossible to please him & others or myself: to separate our Interests without making him angry or unite them without making myself miserable: His Employments, his Inclinations, his Connexions & mode of living are so different from my own that there is no way to preserve that Harmony there is & should be betwixt us, but by

---

[62.] Ibid.
[63.] 'Burials', Part III, *The Parish Register*. See Crabbe, *Poetical Works*, 1932, p. 77.
[64.] Ainger, 1903, p. 40.

our Separation [...] I love my father, but I have other Duties & stronger Affection & cannot give up these tho' I could many things, to his pleasure –[65]

Crabbe could well also have been thinking of his father when he later wrote these lines (in *The Borough*, 1810), in the voice of Peter Grimes:

My father's spirit – he who always tried
To give me trouble, when he lived and died –[66]

And yet, in a sign of that fragile 'harmony' between father and son, the older Crabbe was clearly proud of his son's literary achievements – and readily admitted that he had underrated his son's poetic abilities:

The old man now gloried in the boldness of his adventure, and was proud of its success: he fondly transcribed 'The Library' with his own hand; and, in short, reaped the reward of his own early exertions to give his son a better education than his circumstances could well afford.[67]

Wary of the strain of domestic circumstances with his father, Crabbe went to stay with his sister who was also living in Aldeburgh – as he had previously when serving as the parish doctor. He would also regularly see his brother, Robert, then living in Southwold, eighteen miles up the coast to the north. They would meet at a pub, the White Hart, in the village of Blythburgh on the river Blyth. This was a convenient spot between their two homes for a glass of punch and is best known today – as probably then – for Holy Trinity Church, in which a jack o'the clock (a chiming automaton dating from 1681) bears the inscription: 'As the hours pass away, So doth the life of man decay'.

Many of Crabbe's own passing hours were dedicated to seeing his fiancée, Sarah Elmy, at Parham, where among the Tovells Crabbe could now hold his head high, free from taunts about his 'damned learning.

Yet notwithstanding his literary success and new profession, Crabbe's reception back in his native town was hostile. It truly was a case, his son comments, that – in Jesus's words – 'a prophet is not without honour,

---

[65.] Letter to Edmund Burke, 9 October 1781. See Crabbe, *Letters*, 1985, p. 21.
[66.] 'Peter Grimes', Letter XXII, *The Borough*, 291–92. See Crabbe, *Poems*, 2015, p. 91.
[67.] Crabbe, *Life*, 1947 (1834), p. 91.

Growing to Manhood

save in his own country'. Meanwhile: 'The whisper ran through the town, that a man who had failed in one calling, was not very likely to make a great figure in a new one.'[68]

Adverse stories circulated about the returnee, painting Crabbe 'with not quite clerical decorum', including a rumour that he had been a preacher, when in London, among the Methodists – a charge, were it true, that would have gone down badly with the Anglican establishment. The rumour had its origin in the report of an Aldeburgh sailor who had visited John Wesley's chapel at Moorfields and happened to see Crabbe ascending the pulpit. Like the sailor, Crabbe had visited out of 'pure curiosity', and ended up standing on the steps of the pulpit because the chapel was so crowded.[69] But the misunderstanding was fuel enough for the rumour mill of Aldeburgh, and the slur of dissenter was added to those of lubber and fool.

Crabbe himself was ready to acknowledge where his decorum might have lapsed. When struggling to establish his own medical and apothecary practice in Aldeburgh, he had not been immune to the usual attractions of the town. Perhaps he had overindulged in the taverns, or succumbed to gambling. His son does not specify, simply noting that he fell prey to the snares that beset 'young men early removed from the paternal roof'.[70]

> The juvenile apprentice is, in many respects, too much his own master; and though my father, in his first service, escaped with no worse injury that the association with idle lads generally brings with it, yet, in his second apprenticeship, and afterwards, in the beginning of his own practice at Aldborough, he did not scruple to confess that he was not always proof against the temptations of a town.[71]

Crabbe's weakness for the temptations of a town may have lingered in the memories of some of the churchgoers. For others, the evident change in his station was enough of an inducement to dislike him. It had been less than three years since he left Aldeburgh, and in the estimation of his biographer Alfred Ainger, himself a canon:

---

[68] Ibid, p. 96.
[69] Ibid.
[70] Ibid, p. 94.
[71] Ibid.

> Jealousy of his elevated position and improved fortunes set in with much severity. On the other hand it was more than many could tolerate that the hedge-apothecary of old should be empowered to hold forth in a pulpit.[72]

The pulpit in which Crabbe held forth survives, even if it is not in exactly the same position. 'Big and richly carved', according to Nikolaus Pevsner, with 'oblong panels and arabesques', it was made in 1632 by Charles Warne and James Garrard as a copy of the pulpit in nearby Kelsale.[73] What did Crabbe feel when he stood here and preached for the first time? All that is known is that his sermon, on 20 January 1782, took as its theme the verse: 'Honour all men. Love the brotherhood. Fear God. Honour the king' (1 Peter 2:1). But the congregation seemed not to heed the message. They saw Crabbe as a jumped-up failure, and made their antipathy clear.

'I had been unkindly received in the place,' he complained afterwards. 'I saw unfriendly countenances about me, and, I am sorry to say, I had too much indignation, though mingled, I hope, with better feelings, to care what they thought of me or my sermon.'[74] Neither Crabbe nor his congregation would have believed that the church would one day boast a marble bust of the poet (see Chapter 1); this is to be found close to the stained glass windows designed by John Piper in tribute to Aldeburgh's later son, Benjamin Britten.

Disillusioned by his hostile reception in the church, Crabbe wanted to leave Aldeburgh almost as soon as he arrived. In later life he admitted to his sons that despite the advantage that his clerical position allowed of greater contact with Miss Elmy, his return to Aldeburgh society was far from agreeable.[75] His return had probably been destined from the outset to end in disappointment. His words of foreboding to Burke in October 1781 – just a couple of months before his arrival as curate – show that he was mindful of the misery he had previously suffered, and of the fact that its 'Inhabitants [...] did not use me well'. His early experiences in the pulpit can only have confirmed his misgivings.[76]

[72.] Ainger, 1903, p. 41.
[73.] Nikolaus Pevsner, *The Buildings of England: Suffolk* (London: Penguin Books, 1974), p. 72. Hartley, 2014, p. 5.
[74.] Crabbe, *Life*, 1947 (1834), p. 96.
[75.] Ainger, 1903, p. 41.
[76.] Letter to Edmund Burke, 9 October 1781. See Crabbe, *Letters*, 1985, p. 21.

Figure 10. Pulpit, Church of St Peter and St Paul, Aldeburgh

Crabbe wrote to Lord Thurlow, the Lord Chancellor, who politely suggested that if Crabbe made himself 'capable of preferment', he would try to help him find another position.[77] At the same time, Burke mentioned Crabbe's case to Charles Manners, the fourth Duke of Rutland, whose chaplain was about to retire. By April 1782, Crabbe had received word from Burke that the Duke would appoint him as his domestic chaplain at Belvoir Castle, in Leicestershire, as soon as he could obtain release from his curacies at Aldeburgh. Crabbe was appointed on 12 May and took up his new position in November that year.[78]

Once again, then, Crabbe departed from Aldeburgh – this time for Leicestershire. Soon after his arrival, the Duke of Rutland's family left their Belvoir estate for the London season of March 1783, and would stay in the capital for several months. Crabbe had little to do other than say prayers with the staff, and so had ample time for his writing. By then he had all but completed *The Village*. The poem had been started some years earlier, probably before he left Aldeburgh for London in 1780, and had undergone extensive reworking – much of it under Burke's roof, and with guidance from Samuel Johnson. Through Sir Joshua Reynolds, Crabbe had sent his draft to Johnson, who revised it and wrote back to Reynolds (on 4 March 1783): 'Sir, – I have sent you back Mr Crabbe's poem, which I read with great delight. It is original, vigorous and elegant.'

Johnson concluded portentously: 'I do not doubt of Mr Crabbe's success.'[79]

[77.] Crabbe, *Life*, 1947 (1834), p. 97. Cf. Mitford, 1834, p. 258: 'Lord Thurlow did nothing.' It was Thurlow, however, who in March 1783 provided Crabbe with two small livings in Dorsetshire.

[78.] Thomas Edward Kebbel. *Life of George Crabbe* (London: Walter Scott, 1888), p. 35.

[79.] Samuel Johnson, letter to Sir Joshua Reynolds, 4 March 1783. See Crabbe, *Life*, 1947 (1834), p. 104.

Chapter 3

Domesticity and Botanising

Crabbe's Middle Years

Belvoir and Stathern: The very happiest years in his life

The Village was published in May 1783 to formidable acclaim. It was radical: a critique of the prevailing idealisation of rural life and, by implication, of writers such as Oliver Goldsmith whose extended poem *The Deserted Village* (1770) had offered a sentimental vision of the rural past.[1] Crabbe's starkly realistic depiction won praise in leading journals, leading to rapid and extensive sales. The Duke and Duchess of Rutland, too, were supporters of their new chaplain's literary ambitions. The poet's reputation was sealed.

This also meant that Crabbe, twenty-nine, felt finally able to propose to Sarah Elmy, three years his senior, after an engagement of some eleven years. They were married on 15 December that year, back in Suffolk, in the majestic church of St Michael's at Beccles – a building 'not easily forgotten', according to Nikolaus Pevsner, thanks to its colossal free-standing bell tower and commanding position above the river Waveney.[2] The ceremony was conducted by the Reverend Peter Routh.

---

[1] Albeit one not free of political critique: Goldsmith had indicted ruling-class thefts of English and Irish common lands. On Goldsmith's poetry versus Crabbe's, see Powell, 2004, pp. 91–92.
[2] Pevsner, 1972, p. 91.

The newly-weds spent some eighteen months in apartments at Belvoir Castle (since rebuilt in the Gothic Revival style), where Crabbe had been living since Burke secured him the chaplaincy to the Duke of Rutland. As recorded by the *Dictionary of Irish Biography*, Rutland was popular among both the aristocracy and the people, 'noted for his drinking, gambling, and convivial lifestyle' and 'renowned for both the quality of his dinners and the beauty of his wife'.[3] The family were mostly away during this period, not only for the London season but also because, in December 1783, the Duke – a politician as well as an eminent socialite – was promoted by the Prime Minister William Pitt the Younger to the post of lord lieutenant of Ireland.

The Crabbes found it awkward to be in residence with only the servants at the castle. The advice given to John – the young poet in 'The Patron' (*Tales*, 1812) – is thought to be born of Crabbe's uncomfortable experiences in the household, where he found himself caught between the servants and the nobility, while being of neither:

> Hard, Boy, thy task, to steer thy way among
> That servile, supple, shrewd, insidious throng;
> Who look upon thee as of doubtful race,
> An interloper, one who wants a place:[4]

In the end, Crabbe took a vacant curacy about four miles away at the village of Stathern, moving in the summer of 1785 into the parsonage next to the church of St Guthlac. Belvoir had perhaps become tainted by unhappy associations – Sarah had given birth to a baby during their time there, but the child had died soon after being born. In the next four years at Stathern there were three more children – two sons, George (born 1785, later to be the poet's biographer), John (born 1787), and a daughter, Sarah Susannah, born in 1789, who also died in infancy.

The change of location was welcome. Alfred Ainger recounts being told by a friend, the Reverend J.W. Taylor – rector at Stathern from 1866 – that the villagers' memories of Crabbe included that he spoke 'through his nose', which Ainger takes as a comment on his marked Suffolk accent – and also that he was 'peppery of temper'. One youthful

---

[3] 'Manners, Charles', contributed by Patrick M. Geoghegan: https://www.dib.ie/biography/manners-charles-a5433.
[4] 'The Patron', Tale V, *Tales*, 365–68. See Crabbe, *Poems*, 2015, p. 166.

Domesticity and Botanising

couple who had presented themselves for holy matrimony were driven from the altar, Crabbe scornfully telling them that he had come to marry 'men and women, and not lads and wenches!'[5]

Crabbe used to recount to his children that 'the four years at Stathern were, on the whole, the very happiest in his life'.[6] In *The Village*, he seems almost to anticipate the idyllic state he would achieve in Stathern, evoking those moments of bliss that leaven rural existence:

> *I too must yield, that oft amid these woes*
> *Are gleams of transient mirth and hours of sweet repose.*
> *Such as you find on younger sportive Green,*
> *The 'Squire's tall gate, and churchway-walk between;*
> *Where loitering stray a little tribe of friends*
> *On a fair Sunday when the sermon ends:*[7]

Yet the prevailing voice of the poem – its evocation of a 'frowning coast / Which can no groves nor happy valleys boast' – shows the hold that Aldeburgh and the East Anglian coast retained on Crabbe. As Neil Powell has argued, Crabbe proclaimed himself the kind of poet that he was – an advocate of the poor who disdained to conceal 'real ills' beneath the 'tinsel trappings of poetic pride'. This was precisely because of his origins on a wild coastline. He was, as the opening lines of *The Village* assert, a man of Suffolk – not a silver-tongued Augustan.[8]

If anything, his feelings about his birthplace seem to have deepened in the time he spent away. One day, when he had not seen the sea for more than three years, he rode from Stathern right across Lincolnshire to have a swim, as his son records:

> It was, I think, in the summer of 1787, that my father was seized, one fine summer's day, with so intense a longing to see the sea, from which he had never before been so long absent, that he mounted his horse, rode alone to the coast of Lincolnshire, sixty miles from his house, dipped in the waves that washed the beach of Aldborough, and returned to Stathern.[9]

[5.] Ainger, 1903, p. 61.
[6.] Ibid.
[7.] *The Village*, Book II, 3–8. See Crabbe, 2015, p. 15.
[8.] See Powell, 2004, p. 93.
[9.] Crabbe, *Life*, 1947 (1834), p. 117.

The story is a vivid indication of the lure that Suffolk exercised. Like many a writer and artist after him – most recently Maggi Hambling in her series of sea paintings, the products of long hours of studying the waves – Crabbe was fascinated by the sea. Something of his feelings about 'the waves that washed the beach' at Aldeburgh can be gleaned from lines he wrote twenty years later in *The Borough* (1810):

> *Various and vast, Sublime in all its forms*
> *When lull'd by zephyrs, or when roused by storms,*
> *Its colours changing, when from clouds and sun*
> *Shades after shades jump on its surface run;*
> *Embrown'd and horrid now, and now serene,*
> *In limpid blue, and evanescent green;*[10]

A year before that summer's day trip, Crabbe's father had died – in June 1786. Crabbe had not seen him for years. They had become estranged after his father's second marriage in June 1782 to Mary Revett, a widow from nearby Wickham Market, two years after the death of Crabbe's mother. Mary Revett had brought home 'several children by a former husband' and 'the house became still more uncomfortable than it had for many years before been to the members of his own family'.[11] The remarriage provoked an irredeemable break with his eldest son.

But Crabbe's ties with Aldeburgh remained unsevered, not least because in October 1786, his sister Mary married Thomas Sparkes, a local builder, in Aldeburgh church, and returned to live there from Ipswich – where she had gone to work as a milliner in 1782. Over the next three years, Crabbe made several brief trips to Suffolk, but the first extended visit was from mid September until early November 1790 (on which occasion Crabbe preached at churches in the vicinity). His son, then five years old, recalls the journey in their huge old gig: 'Sometimes, as we proceeded, my father read aloud; sometimes he left us for a while to botanise among the hedgerows, and returned with some unsightly weed or bunch of moss, to him precious.'[12]

Despite these opportunities to botanise, the years after the appearance of *The Village* in 1783 were arid from the point of view of published works. After 1785, when *The Newspaper* was published, Crabbe was not

---

[10] 'General Description', Letter I, *The Borough*. See Crabbe, *Poetical Works*, 1932, p. 111.

[11] Crabbe, *Life*, 1947 (1834), p. 119.

[12] Crabbe, *Life*, 1947 (1834), p. 122. See also Crabbe, *Letters*, 1985, p. 41.

to be in print again for more than twenty years – until 1807. Rather it was a period of domesticity: parish work, a growing family and, of course, indulging his passion for natural history. Crabbe continued to write, but 'from his thirty-first year to his fifty-second, he buried himself completely in the obscurity of domestic and village life' and was never seen '(unless in company) seated in a chair, enjoying what is called a lounge – that is to say, doing nothing. Out of doors he had always some object in view – a flower, or a pebble, or his notebook, in his hand; and in the house, if he was not writing, he was reading.'[13]

The autumn of 1787 brought the sudden and untimely death of his friend and patron, the Duke of Rutland, at the age of only thirty-three, having succumbed to alcoholic liver disease. The Duke left behind a widow and six children. The Duchess was keen to keep her husband's *protégé* in the neighbourhood. She gave him a letter for Lord Thurlow, the Lord Chancellor, asking that the two small Dorset livings that the Lord Chancellor had given Crabbe in March 1783 be exchanged for two of superior value in the Vale of Belvoir.

Lord Thurlow initially turned Crabbe down, but later acceded to the Duchess's request and Crabbe was presented with the two livings – Muston in Leicestershire and Allington in Lincolnshire. They were both within sight of Belvoir Castle and no more than a mile apart. To hold the livings required dispensation from the Archbishop of Canterbury, and a degree – which Crabbe did not have. To get round this, he sat what was called a 'Lambeth degree', a single examination at Lambeth Palace. On 10 January 1789, he was granted the ecclesiastical degree of Bachelor of Laws. At last, his learning – derided by John Tovell, championed by Edmund Burke – had earned an official seal.

And so Crabbe became a rector in his own parish, Muston, leaving Stathern on 25 February 1789, the year of the French Revolution. It was an important moment in his career; but his new position was not to be for long. Within three years, in 1792, came news of the death of John Tovell, Sarah's uncle. Crabbe was busy with the task of enclosing a new garden for botanic specimens when he was summoned to Parham as executor. The estate fell to Sarah's mother and her elderly spinster sister, Miss Tovell, although in due course Crabbe, through his wife, was to inherit the house. He decided to place a curate at Muston and move to Parham.

[13.] Ibid, pp. 114–15.

The move earned him enemies: here he was, leaving the Vale of Belvoir because his family had the option of inhabiting a better house back in his native Suffolk. His son recounts an "ominous" beginning to their new life: "As we were slowly quitting the place, preceded by our furniture, a stranger, though one who knew my father's circumstances, called out in an impressive tone: 'You are wrong, you are wrong.'" The admonition, he suggests, found an echo in Crabbe's own conscience, and "during the whole journey seemed to ring in his ears like a supernatural voice."[14]

Parham and Glemham:
A family walk through the green lanes

Parham regained was an unhappy time for the Crabbe family. They arrived at the small village – once the scene of Crabbe's courtship of Sarah – in October 1792. The death of John Tovell, and the pervasive atmosphere of grief at Ducking Hall, at once produced tensions: 'Mrs Tovell [John's widow] and her sister-in-law [the spinster Miss Tovell], sitting by the fireside weeping, did not even rise up to welcome my parents,' Crabbe's son recalls, 'but uttered a few chilling words, and wept again. Our arrival in Suffolk was by no means palatable to all my mother's relations.'[15]

The froideur was such that soon after the family's arrival, the Crabbes went to stay for several months – during the early part of 1793 – with his sister and brother-in-law, Mary and Thomas Sparkes, in Aldeburgh. The eldest boys were placed under the tuition of one of the 'dames' in Aldeburgh who had taught Crabbe.

When Crabbe finally returned to the Tovell household in Parham, it was to take on the office of curate-in-charge at the nearby Sweffling parish on behalf of the incumbent, the Reverend Richard Turner. This picturesque church and its hilltop graveyard would later inspire John Cowper Powys to write: 'There is a spirit in these ancient stones, / These grassy mounds and immemorial trees / That scarce seems conscious of the passing breeze' (*Sonnet written in Sweffling Churchyard*, 1899).

It was a fortunate move for Crabbe: the Reverend Turner became a mentor – described by Crabbe's son as 'my father's most intimate friend and chosen critic'. The son writes moreover that 'one of the chief

---

[14.] Crabbe, *Life*, 1947 (1834), p. 130.
[15.] Crabbe, *Life*, 1947 (1834), p. 130.

sources of comfort all through my father's residence in Suffolk was his connection with this honoured man. He considered his judgment a sure safeguard and reliance in all cases practical and literary'.[16]

Soon after, a second curacy fell to Crabbe – that of Great Glemham, a medieval parish located between the towns of Framlingham and Saxmundham. The name is thought to derive from the Old English *gleam*, 'merriment'; but it was not a time of great merriment for Crabbe. Perhaps his only joy in Parham, where he would remain for four years, was in the landscape. The village lies in the agricultural river valley of the upper Ore. The Suffolk Sandlings, a heathland terrain bounding much of the coast, were within walking distance, and gave Crabbe ample opportunity to pursue his botanical passion. In a letter of 1794 to Edmund Cartwright, a fellow priest and botanist (whose father, also called Edmund and a close friend of Crabbe's, invented the power loom that revolutionised the process of weaving), Crabbe keenly described the coastal sandlings and the vegetation at Aldeburgh:

> Almost all the Coast, however uninteresting in Appearance has in it, Stores for the Botanist & natural Historian in general: A more flat, uniform & Tame District can scarsely be imagined than that part of the Suffolk Shore opposite to my present Habitation. ...
>
> I was observing the progress of the Vegetation on the Beach At Aldborough in Suff. where the Sea had a few years since overflown, & where the Stones were nearly bare or partially covered with a little light Sand blown from the neibouring Banks. Here I found the Pisum maritimum, the Chelidonium glaucium, the Statice Armeria & several other harty & frugal plants which live on little & thrust their roots far in the Soil in search of Food, but among these I was struck with the more than usual Number of Trefoils & some of them the very scarser kinds which grown almost on one Spot on this bare & || nearly || barren Surface.[17]

[16.] Ibid, p. 144. See also p. 145: 'While at Glemham, as at Parham, my father rarely visited any neighbours except Mr North and his brother Mr Long; nor did he often receive any visitors. But one week in every year was to him, and to all his household, a period of peculiar enjoyment – that during which he had Mr Turner for his guest.'

[17.] Letter to Edmund Cartwright Jr., 22 July 1794. See Crabbe, *Letters*, 1985, p. 55, p. 57.

Poring over the sparse vegetation in the 'bare and barren' sand, Crabbe even thought he had discovered a new plant:

> A light Sand constitutes the Surface, and you are obliged to look minutely before you be able to discover any vegetable Cloathing in many parts of it. It was to this Coast I alluded in some verses I wrote [Crabbe is referring to lines in *The Village*] wherein I spoke of the poppy, Mallow, Darnel & Bugloss as the few ornaments (& those Ornaments of Sterility) which the Soil could boast of: It is however my Fortune, in some measure to sing (at least to say) a Recantation; for this dispised place has afforded me much Amusement & not that only, but has impowered me, (so far as I know at present) to introduce to the botanical world a new Species of British plant, or rather a new Species speaking more generally, for I can neither find it in the Flora of [*conj.leaf*] these Kingdoms nor the Species plantarum of the last & enlarged Editions.[18]

But no doubt to his great disappointment, Crabbe came to discover that the plant, a species of trefoil, had already been identified a year before by a Mr Lillywigg at Great Yarmouth, and exhibited at a meeting of the Linnean Society in May 1793. It was the *Trifolium suffocatum*, or 'Suffocated Clover'.[19]

Undeterred, he went on to produce a botanical treatise in English, drawing upon his coastal walks as well as his time in Leicestershire. Unfortunately, this was another botanical ambition to be thwarted: the treatise ended up on a bonfire in one of Crabbe's 'incremations in Parham', after he sought the opinion of a friend, John Davies, vice-master of Trinity College, Cambridge. Davies told him that he 'could not stomach the notion of degrading such a science by treating of it in a modern language' – Latin being the only language that would do.[20]

Crabbe's rambling and scientific exploits aside, the years at Parham were in general miserable – marred by the deaths of two more children. The family death toll, commonplace at the time, seems shocking today. The Crabbes' first child had been born at Belvoir and only lived a few hours. The couple then had George, in 1785, John Waldron, in 1787, and Sarah Susannah, baptised in Muston in 1789. She died that same year

---

[18] Ibid, pp. 55–56.
[19] Letter to Edmund Cartwright Jr., 3 February 1795. Ibid, p. 62, n. 4.
[20] Crabbe, *Life*, 1947 (1834), p. 116.

Domesticity and Botanising

and was buried there. Edmund, a third boy, was baptised at Muston on 25 January 1790. The following year another daughter, Sarah, was baptised in September 1791, and died in infancy.

That was not the end of the family's tragic losses: with the family now at Parham, another son – the youngest of the family, William, was baptised on 10 October 1792. But not quite a year later he was to be buried in the churchyard, on 6 September 1793. Then, just three years on, the family suffered a further death – that of Edmund, William's older brother. He died aged six at Parham and was buried there on 11 March 1796.[21]

There had been seven children born and now there were two. The cumulative losses – and particularly that of Edmund – affected Sarah so severely that the Crabbes decided they had to leave Parham and its associations of grief. Her sufferings triggered what is now believed to have been severe bipolar disorder, and a mental decline from which she would suffer until her death in 1813.

In the village, there was also the problem that John Tovell had been gregarious and well liked and Crabbe was not. Something of the unpopularity he had suffered among the churchgoers of Aldeburgh seems to have followed him inland. Ducking Hall, later altered to become Parham Lodge (see Chapter 2), was no longer the convivial place and focus of village life that it had been when Tovell was alive. In a letter of 1795 to the younger Cartwright, Crabbe admitted: 'I do not believe that Sundays excepted, I have been four paces from my House this Winter. If it were not a season when all Vegetation slumbers, I should say we vegetate rather than live. At any Time our Society is contracted but in this part of the year the few Friends we have, being greater people than ourselves, are in Town and we know nothing of mankind, but from Letters and Newspapers.'[22]

And yet despite such indications of his reclusive and undemonstrative personality – at least so far as Parham society went – Crabbe's close friendships were strong and enduring. He received kindness and support at this time from friends such as Dudley North (formerly Dudley Long), the prominent Whig politician who had in 1789 inherited the manor of nearby Little Glemham Hall. It was North who had helped him twelve

---

[21.] Crabbe, *Letters*, 1985, footnote 41. Both William and Edmund are believed to have been buried in Parham churchyard but many of the inscriptions on the older graves are now obliterated.

[22.] Letter to Edmund Cartwright Jr., 3 February 1795. See Crabbe, *Letters*, 1985, p. 60.

years earlier, when he desperately needed money to try his fortunes in London. Crabbe was regularly invited to dine at North's table, and renewed contact with various members of the Whig party whom he had known through Burke – a group, as Neil Powell suggests, 'much more to Crabbe's taste than the Duke of Rutland's predominantly Tory circle'.[23]

Nowadays commonly referred to simply as Glemham Hall, North's house was – and is – a relic of the Elizabethan era, built in 1560 amid 300 acres of parkland. North's father had transformed the property between 1717 and 1722, creating the impressive Georgian frontage – a three-storey facade with projecting wings – that is visible today from the A12 road. The gabled Elizabethan rear is likewise much as Crabbe would have recognised it as he walked in his friend's garden.

North was to come to Crabbe's rescue again. Within a few months of the death of Edmund, it happened that a separate property belonging to North and his brother Charles Long, Great Glemham Hall, fell vacant. Despite the name, this house was more modest than Little Glemham Hall, the 'Little' and 'Great' referring to the villages rather than the respective properties.

Crabbe was offered the tenancy at a greatly reduced rent. He had already, at North's invitation, assumed the curacy at the fourteenth-century church of All Saints, Great Glemham, two year earlier – and so he knew the village. The family moved into Great Glemham Hall in October 1796. Crabbe's son recalls: 'The situation was delightful in itself, and extremely convenient for the clerical duties my father had to perform.' He adds: 'Never can I cease to look back to my days at Glemham as the golden spot of my existence.'[24]

Crabbe himself wrote in more exigent terms at the time of the move:

> In October I purpose to remove to North Glemham where my Friend Mr North having one [house] now Empty, will accommode me & in which (much as even rational Hope, has deceived me) I will hope for a little Repose; and with so much more prospect of Success as it increases the Distance between us and some malignant Spirit who has taken the Form of a woman indeed, but no other Disguise whatever.[25]

[23.] Powell, 2004, p. 140. Cf. Ainger, 1903, p. 73.

[24.] Crabbe, *Life*, 1947 (1834), p. 134.

[25.] Letter to Edmund Cartwright Jr., 7 July 1796. See Crabbe, *Letters*, 1985, p. 67.

Domesticity and Botanising

Figure 11. All Saints Church, Great Glemham

The malignant spirit he unrestrainedly describes was the sister of John Tovell, Elizabeth, who was still living at Ducking Hall. His comment gives an insight into the tensions that had persisted at the Tovell household in Parham ever since the cool reception of the Crabbe family in 1792. At Ducking Hall, Crabbe had complained (in a letter to Cartwright in summer 1793) that:

I am neither Master of the House, nor Guest. Mrs Crabbe neither Commands nor obeys: The Servants are neither ours nor any other persons. [...] In short This is nobody's House *and* Nobody governs, nobody obeys; nobody is satisfied, but Everybody agrees that is a miserable place & joins in hope that it will be better.[26]

Great Glemham Hall represented an escape from this misery of uncertain standing. The house in which the Crabbes lived no longer survives, like most of his homes; but it is possible to imagine – from the younger Crabbe's reminiscences alone – a place of elegance and tranquillity, bringing that hoped-for 'little Repose'.

The house was situated just a couple of miles from Parham, in the picturesque heart of Great Glemham Park. It had been built in 1708 and was inhabited before Crabbe by a certain Lady Harbord. The Crabbes were to stay until 1801, when the Longs sold the estate to Dr Samuel Kilderbee. In 1814 he demolished and rebuilt the house. (Crabbe's son records that the old house was 'levelled to the ground'. A new and elegant Mansion has been built on the hill by Dr. (Samuel) Kilderbee.' Kilderbee, a churchman and lawyer, had been the great friend of painter Thomas Gainsborough since the latter's Ipswich days in the 1750s.)

Kilderbee's replacement mansion, known nowadays as Great Glemham House, is an edifice in grey brick – square, stately, robustly Georgian – standing on a slightly different site from the house that Crabbe lived in. Crabbe's property 'stood at the bottom of the park near the village', according to John Mitford in his 1834 review for *The Gentleman's Magazine*.[27]

But the original Great Glemham Hall was nonetheless the 'most splendid house that the family ever occupied', Crabbe's son recounts. The '*lares* were removed from Parham, where they had always been unpropitious, to this beautiful residence, where my parents remained for four or five years, to their entire satisfaction.'[28]

[26.] Crabbe, *Letters*, 1985, letter 25 to Edmund Cartwright, Jun. Parham. 4 September 1793, p. 53

[27.] Mitford, 1834, p. 259. Cf. Earl of Cranbrook, 'George Crabbe and Great Glemham', *Proceedings of the Suffolk Institute of Archaeology and Natural History*, Vol. 15, No. 1 (1949): pp. 116–17 – an article that debates the vexed question of the houses' respective locations. Kilderbee's erection stood at the summit of the sloping park, in grounds that were remodelled by Humphrey Repton: Powell, 2004, p. 146.

[28.] Crabbe, *Life*, 1947 (1834), p. 134.

Domesticity and Botanising

The younger Crabbe, aged eleven at the time of the move, paints a lyrical picture of the family's days there: 'The summer evenings especially, at this place, dwell on my memory like a delightful dream.' After lessons, they would walk through the green lanes around Glemham:

> Along these we wandered sometimes till the moon had risen, my mother leading a favourite little niece who lived with us, my father reading some novel aloud, while my brother and I caught moths or other insects to add to his collection. ...
>
> When it was too dark to see, he would take a battledore and join us in the pursuit of moths, or carry his little favourite if she were tired, and so we proceeded homeward while on the right and left, before and behind, the nightingales (I never heard so many among those woods) were pouring out their melody, sometimes three or four at once.[29]

In the winter evenings, in place of rustic excursions, Crabbe read to the family: 'He read in that natural and easy manner, that permits the whole attention to be given to the subject.'[30] All the while he was still busy writing. The poet's younger son, John, records that while searching for and examining plants or insects, he 'was moulding verses into measure and smoothness'.[31] He taught himself French and Italian, and continued with his botanical and entomological studies. The older son, George, adds: 'I rather think, indeed, that this was, of his whole life, the period during which he carried the greatest and most indefatigable zeal into his researches in Natural History.'[32]

In this time at Glemham, Crabbe turned his hand to prose. He completed three novels but all were destroyed in the same incrematory spirit he had displayed with the *English Treatise on Botany* in Parham. His wife Sarah, commenting on a passage from one of the novels, remarked that 'the effect [was] very inferior to that of the corresponding pieces in verse.' Upon hearing this, Crabbe paused in his reading and – after reflection – conceded: 'Your remark is just.'[33]

[29.] Ibid, p. 136.
[30.] Ibid, p. 137.
[31.] Memorandum quoted in ibid, pp. 140–41.
[32.] Ibid, p. 141.
[33.] Ibid, p. 143.

Fatherhood and domesticity, plants and insects, walking in green lanes – these were the other main occupations of Crabbe in rural Suffolk. It was a tranquil interlude in which he was preparing to delve back in his writings into the grimmer experiences of his childhood.

Rendham: The final Suffolk years

Crabbe's time in Suffolk, the place that had drawn him back in time and again between his ventures into the world, was nearing a close.

Around the turn of the century, there was a crackdown on the habit of clergymen living outside their parishes. In July 1800, the Bishop of Lincoln, Dr George Pretyman, informed all his absentee clergymen that if they were not residing at their benefices (in Crabbe's case, Muston in Leicestershire and Allington in Lincolnshire), they must give the reasons in writing. Crabbe, who had left Leicestershire following the death of Sarah's uncle, John Tovell, had no wish to return, and yet he was reluctant to lose the sinecures he had been granted after his four years in Stathern on the Duke of Rutland's death.

Crabbe also felt a 'strong partiality to Suffolk'.[34] Relatives on both sides of the family lived in close proximity – even if he had lamented that fact in the case of Sarah's aunt, Elizabeth Tovell. But he was also thinking of the interests and education of his sons, as well as his wife. And so he persuaded Dudley North to intervene on his behalf with the powers that were, with the result that North managed to obtain a four-year extension to his leave of absence from Leicestershire.

Another problem swiftly arose, however – this time of North's making. In 1801, he and his brother Charles Long agreed to sell Great Glemham Hall, in which the Crabbes had been happily ensconced for four years, and to divide the proceeds. And so, in October of that year, the family was compelled to move to the neighbouring village of Rendham.

A small settlement with two village greens, Rendham lies on the River Alde where it meets with the Gull before the latter diverts to Sweffling. The village dates from Roman times: the first inhabitants are believed to have settled in the first century AD, drawn by the sustenance that the river provided. In AD 60, Queen Boudicca ruled this area of Suffolk as leader of the Iceni, some twenty years into the Roman conquest of

---

[34.] Crabbe, *Life*, 1947 (1834), p. 146.

Domesticity and Botanising

Britain under the Emperor Claudius, which had begun in AD 43. It is thought that the villagers joined her army and took part in the storming of the temple of Claudius in Colchester.

In 1907, two Rendham schoolboys found a metal object in the mud of the River Alde. It turned out to be one of the most significant Roman artefacts unearthed in Britain – a hollow bronze head of Claudius, looted by the Iceni from Colchester, where it was probably hacked off the body of a larger (possibly equestrian) statue. The hollow eye sockets would once have contained pieces of enamel or glass; but in its surviving state, the vacant-eyed head is not unlike the classicising countenance of Crabbe's portrait bust in Aldeburgh church. It is now in the British Museum.

Rendham boasts another relic – the only surviving house of all the properties that the Crabbes occupied, the others having been variously razed and replaced. It is a stuccoed Georgian dwelling at the foot of a meadow in the Alde Valley, smaller than Ducking Hall or Great Glemham Hall – a 'much more unpretending house' in the words of Huchon – and close to the new parsonage (now known as the Old Rectory). Since at least the nineteenth century, it has mainly gone by the name of Lady Whincup's house.[35] A pale yellow property set in peaceful surroundings, it has been extended since Crabbe's lifetime – but the Georgian core remains intact. A blue plaque records that the poet lived there.[36]

Little else is known of this time. Crabbe appears to have thrown his energies into parish work while enjoying the humdrum domesticity of life in Rendham and the diversion of his writing, with occasional visits to Aldeburgh or Muston. His main concern in these years was the

---

[35] Huchon, 1907, p. 198. Cf. Mitford, 1834, pp. 198–99.

[36] The house stands in the dip of rolling landscape just outside Rendham. The present owner, Carl Locri, kindly allowed the author access to the house, including the main reception rooms on either side of the main front door. They are of typical elegant Georgian proportions with original fireplaces. The Old Rectory stands to the north of Lady Whincup's house, on the other side of the B1120. According to Locri, 'Lady Whincup's land ownership used to stretch across the B1120 – so at that time we were adjacent landowners.' The house for some years was known as Grove House. In 1954 the Aldeburgh Music Society celebrated Crabbe's bicentenary and restored the name to Lady Whincup's. The blue plaque was installed at that time.

Figure 12. St Michael's Church, Rendham

Figure 13. Lady Whincup's House, Rendham

Figure 14. St Mary's Church, Parham

education of his two sons, and the expense of seeing them both through Cambridge; the older son, George, the future biographer, was to go up to the university in 1803.[37]

Writing some forty years later, the critic John Mitford observed that Crabbe had been 'exceedingly liked and respected' during his years back in Suffolk: '"Parson Crabbe" is talked of to this day by all the elder people in all the villages from Aldborough to Glemham; – by the farmers for his frank and friendly simplicity; and by the wives and daughters for his elegant attentions, and engaging courtesy.'[38] The family stayed in Rendham some four years, until 1805, and during that time *The Parish Register* was all but completed (to be published in 1807 as part of *Poems*), and *The Borough* begun.

While Crabbe's middle years might appear a fallow chapter, he was collecting observations and experiences, much as he gathered botanical specimens on his walks. As he explained (with a certain ironic detachment) in his autobiographical sketch of 1816, *The Parish Register* had grown out of the facts of his daily circumstances:

> Why our author should so long abstain from any call or claim upon public favour, it is not our business to enquire; but it is most probable that the subject itself, viz. Village Manners, described under the three parts of a parish register – Births, Marriages, and Burials, and the further opportunities which he had of viewing these in the different places wherein he resided, gave the hope of success in this attempt. He must have acquired some knowledge of men and their manners; and if from disuse his facility of versification was somewhat abated, his powers of discrimination, and his accuracy in describing, were proportionately augmented.[39]

The Crabbes returned to the parsonage at Muston in Leicestershire in August 1805. They had been away in Suffolk for thirteen years: four at Parham, five at Great Glemham, and four at Rendham. Suffolk had, in this time, sown the seeds of the poet's greatest works.

---

[37] Powell, 2004, p. 157.
[38] Mitford, 1834, p. 259.
[39] Crabbe, 1816, p. 516.

Chapter 4

Religion and Politics

Crabbe and religion: Without a little Latin, we should have made nothing of you

Here, on a Sunday eve, when service ends,
Meet and rejoice a family of friends;
All speak aloud, are happy and are free,
And glad they seem, and gaily they agree.[1]

Crabbe became a popular preacher during his Suffolk years, despite the cool reception he had received in Aldeburgh in 1781. He enjoyed large congregations and would have cut a familiar figure in the various pulpits of the county, including those of St Peter and St Paul in Aldeburgh, St Mary the Virgin in Parham – where the family lived between 1792 and 1796 – St Mary the Virgin in Sweffling, All Saints in Great Glemham (1796–1801), and St Michael's in Rendham (1801–05).

The content of Crabbe's sermons, as much as their style, seems to have been a balance of idealism and realism, poise and informality. He was 'deemed a gospel preacher', that is, 'a minister who urges his flock to virtuous conduct, by placing a future award ever full in their view, instead of dwelling on the temporal motives rendered so prominent at

---

[1.] 'Baptisms', Part I, *The Parish Register*. See Crabbe, *Poetical Works*, 1932, p. 52.

that time by many of his brethren'.[2] In other words, he did not urge the doing of good works so as to secure some present benefit. His son records that:

> His style of reading in the desk was easy and natural – at any rate, natural to him, though a fastidious ear might find in it a species of affectation, something a little like assumed authority; but there was no tone, nothing of singsong.

Crabbe's style was certainly down to earth by the standards of the time, notwithstanding its subtle grain of 'assumed authority'. He did not stand on ceremony and actively disliked rhetorical posturing.

> In the pulpit he was entirely unaffected; read his sermon with earnestness, and in a voice and manner, on some occasions, peculiarly affecting; but he made no attempt at extemporaneous preaching, and utterly disregarded all the mechanism of oratory.

As his son continues, he had that trait, 'very desirable in a minister', of plain speaking and easy candour – a characteristic that amounted to 'the most complete exemption from fear or solicitude'. On a tithe day, he would announce – stepping from the pulpit – 'I must have some money, gentlemen.'[3] On occasion, if it grew dark, he would abruptly end his sermon, declaring: 'Upon my word I cannot see; I must give you the rest when we meet again.' Or he might move to a pew near the window, stand on the seat, and finish his sermon from this felicitous vantage point 'with the most admirable indifference to the remarks of his congregation'.[4]

One can glimpse a touch of autobiography in the character of the Author-Rector in *The Parish Register* (1807), a figure somewhat aloof – absorbed in learned questions – and yet indifferent to rank or status, and undiscriminating in his kindnesses:

> *Then came the Author-Rector: his delight*
> *Was all in books; to read them, or to write:*
> *Women and men he strove alike to shun,*

---

[2] Crabbe, *Life*, 1947 (1834), p. 139.
[3] Ibid. Cf. Mitford, 1834, p. 259.
[4] Crabbe, *Life*, 1947 (1834), p. 140.

And hurried homeward when his tasks were done:
Courteous enough, but careless what he said,
For points of learning he reserved his head;
And when addressing either poor or rich,
He knew no better than his cassock which:
He, like an osier, was of pliant kind,
Erect by nature, but to bend inclined;
Not like a creeper falling to the ground,
Or meanly catching on the neighbours round: –
Careless was he of surplice, hood, and band, –
And kindly took them as they came to hand:
Nor, like the doctor, wore a world of hat,
As if he sought for dignity in that:
He talk'd, he gave, but not with cautious rules: –
Nor turn'd from gipsies, vagabonds, or fools;
It was his nature, but they thought it whim,
And so our beaux and beauties turn'd from him:[5]

Perhaps the 'beaux and beauties' of Suffolk's parishes, such as they were, looked askance at their bookish and unpretentious churchman. But other parishioners warmed to him. At Great Glemham, he took the congregation plant-hunting after the service, corralling them into one of the botanical rambles that had so often been his solitary pleasure.[6]

As for theological doctrine, Crabbe was decidedly of the centre ground for the majority of his life. The religious opinions that he expressed 'place him firmly in the Broad-Church or latitudinarian tradition,' one historian concludes, 'sceptical regarding the evangelical spirit and never attracted to the reviving High-Church movement' – although in later life he did show some leanings towards the thinking of the evangelical Christians of the Church of England. 'Crabbe shows little interest in dogma and theological disputation, but always emphasizes integrity of conviction and the performance of good works.'[7]

---

[5] 'Burials', Part III, *The Parish Register.* See Crabbe, *Poetical Works,* 1932, p. 80.
[6] 'George Crabbe: An English Life, 1754–1832', *Church Times,* 2 November 2006: https://www.churchtimes.co.uk/articles/2004/15-october/books-arts/book-reviews/george-crabbe-an-english-life-1754-1832
[7] Thomas C. Faulkner, 'Introduction' in Crabbe, *Letters,* 1985, p. xxiv.

Throughout his life, Crabbe remained liberal in matters of theology. In 1825, at the age of seventy, he reflected in a letter to the novelist Alethea Lewis (an old friend and correspondent from his earliest Parham days):

> The longer I live, the more I wonder, not that Christians should believe differently and split into Sects, Semi-sects and demi-semi Sects, but that they should be angry with each other: that is strange: If they will but love God & each other I see nothing either wonderful or terrible in their different Modes of receiving the Tidings: they may be glad Tidings to all as I do trust they are to many.[8]

In the view of Thomas C. Faulkner, editor of Crabbe's *Selected Letters and Journals*, the closest that the poet came to an evangelical fervour in religion occurred in the early years of his adult life, when he experienced 'a new birth' in the shape of his fiancée Sarah Elmy (whom he also called Mira and Sally).[9] In a letter of 1776 to Alethea, he referred to Elmy as 'that dear Girl who has been the Instrument of leading me to new Thoughts and purer Desires [...] my Soul was at that Time in Dread & Darkness, deceiving itself and just awakening to light, or rather just awaken'd.'[10]

That early fervour – a compound of romance and religion – appears to have dimmed over the years, particularly as Sarah's mental illness took its toll. In his letter to Alethea of 1825, Crabbe wrote: 'I had long, very long to watch a Being whose Mind was growing cloudy & at last became nearly dark, yet with Coruscations & Strugglings for the Light at times.' His language poignantly evokes and ironically reverses the epiphany described in the earlier letter – that transition from 'Dread & Darkness' into the light of blossoming love. Here, by contrast, he charts the slow, inexorable obscuration of Sarah's mind.

Crabbe's faith seems generally to have been humanistic – rooted in and intertwined with the circumstances and people of his own life, rather than theological abstraction. It is an outlook that can be traced back to his childhood in Aldeburgh, where, attending church, he sat beside his mother in the pew, discerning in her bearing a model of devotion just as inspiring as whatever was issuing from the pulpit.

'Mr Crabbe's early religious impressions were, no doubt, strongly influenced by those of his mother;' his son observes.

[8.] Letter to Alethea Brereton, 1825. Quoted in ibid.
[9.] Ibid, p. xxv.
[10.] Letter to Alethea Brereton, 1776. Quoted in ibid.

> She was, as I have already said, a deeply devout woman; but her seriousness was not of the kind that now almost exclusively receives that designation. [...] doubtless, her mildness, humility, patient endurance of afflictions and sufferings, meek habits, and devout spirit, strongly recommended her example to her son, and impressed his young mind with a deep belief that the principles which led to such practice must be those of the Scriptures of God.[11]

Later, in the years of their courtship and early marriage, Sarah would take the place of Crabbe's mother as his key spiritual influence: 'the influence of Mira, as pious as the Matilda of the *Tales of the Hall*, came at its appointed hour and proved a blessing for the future clergyman. She strengthened his faith and warned him against unprincipled companions.'[12]

While he was away in London, Crabbe would send Sarah detailed accounts of the sermons he had heard, and composed his own prayers. In one case he noted a whole address from memory. His 'Poet's Journal' from London contains, in his son's words, 'evidence of the purity of his conduct, and of the habitual attention he paid to religious topics'.[13]

Above all, it was his patron Burke who set Crabbe on a clerical path, having discovered that his talents lay more in the direction of divinity than medicine. 'It is most fortunate,' Burke told him, 'that your father exerted himself to send you to that second school; without a little Latin we should have made nothing of you: now, I think we shall succeed' (see also Chapter 9). Crabbe's fascination with botany had also undoubtedly helped in furnishing him with the 'little Latin' that an eighteenth-century churchman required – the treatises were written in Latin, like all scientific works. Certainly, he had acquired enough to read and quote the Latin poets, to which he took a great liking – rarely was he without a favourite book of Latin poetry.

But if Crabbe was naturally pious and well read in the scriptures, his youth was certainly not unblemished. He acknowledged a 'lapse' when in Aldeburgh during his second apprenticeship and his son refers to 'dissipations of his earlier manhood'. Whatever Crabbe's libertine days

---

[11.] Crabbe, *Life*, 1947 (1834), pp. 93–94.
[12.] Huchon, 1907, p. 54. Matilda is the virtuous rector's daughter in 'Adventures of Richard Concluded' (Book VI, *Tales of the Hall*) with whom Richard is in love.
[13.] Crabbe, *Life*, 1947 (1834), p. 95.

consisted of, their worst excesses were allayed by the severe illness that struck him down not long after he began as a surgeon-apothecary in Aldeburgh in the mid 1770s. This brush with mortality brought about, as his son recalls, a 'strong and permanent change' – reminiscent of Prince Hal's transformation from waywardness to wisdom.[14]

Crabbe later spoke publicly of this moment of reckoning. In a sermon delivered at Stathern on 27 June 1784, before resettling in Suffolk, he asserted that there is 'with most men a time, commonly an early one, which in a great measure determines their future life, a time when they feel the force and necessity of religion, bear up against their vices, and become virtuous'.[15] He later told his children that he made a solemn resolution following his illness; and those who observed him after his convalescence agreed 'in stating his conduct and conversation to have been that of a regular, temperate and religious young man'.[16]

Crabbe and opium: His long and generally healthy life

Temperate in all things – but even temperateness had its limits. Like many of his contemporaries, Crabbe took opium for much of his life. Samuel Taylor Coleridge, Thomas de Quincey, Lord Byron, John Keats, and Percy Bysshe Shelley all imbibed the drug, taken usually as a tincture in whisky or claret, whether for medicinal or recreational reasons, or both. All the leading Romantic poets, with the exception of William Wordsworth, appear to have used it at some point.

Opium was the panacea of the early nineteenth century, although the drug had been in use since the birth of medicine as a modern profession. A popular aspirin-like analgesic, albeit powerfully addictive, it was recommended for pain of any sort or irritation to the nerves or instability of mood. Crabbe is said to have been prescribed opium – or laudanum – for the first time in 1790, to relieve pain.

Crabbe's son dates his father's opium use to 'soon after 1789' when the family was still in Muston, but Crabbe was making trips to Suffolk. Aged forty-six, he was 'stout and healthy', but clearly there were chinks

---

[14.] Crabbe, *Life*, 1947 (1834), p. 94. Cf. Powell on Crabbe's move to London in 1780: 'He was a young man of twenty-five and on the loose in London, and he is most unlikely to have told everything to his fond and pious fiancée.' Powell, 2004, p. 50.

[15.] Quoted in Huchon, 1907, p. 54.

[16.] Crabbe, *Life*, 1947 (1834), p. 95.

in his robustness. In particular, he suffered from attacks of dizziness or vertigo. When he preached his first sermon at Muston in 1789, Sarah predicted – with undue pessimism – that he would preach very few more. About 1790, when visiting Ipswich on a journey to Suffolk, he suffered 'a most alarming attack'. Crabbe was alone, having left Sarah at an inn as he walked into town, and he suddenly staggered and fell. The episode was attributed by passers-by to inebriation. But he was seen by a Dr Clubbe, who squarely pronounced: 'let the digestive organs bear the whole blame: you must take opiates'.[17]

Crabbe then took the drug for the rest of his life. 'From that time his constituents began to amend rapidly,' his son documents, 'and his constitution was renovated; a rare effect of opium.'[18]

But Dr Clubbe's prescription may not have been Crabbe's first introduction to opium. The drug was ubiquitous as a tranquilliser and painkiller; Thomas de Quincey's *Confessions of an English Opium-Eater*, an account of the raptures and ravages of addiction during this era, would appear in 1821. In its derivative form of laudanum, Crabbe may have had access to the drug back in his Woodbridge days, between 1771 and 1774, when he was a surgeon's apprentice. Or perhaps he experimented with it in London, a decade before his digestive organs apparently failed him in Ipswich.[19]

In *The Library* (1781), published while he was in London, Crabbe likened books to 'mild opiates' of the heart, offering a refuge from life's turbulence:

> *And round the heart and o'er the aching head,*
> *Mild opiates here their sober influence shed.*[20]

Of course, the metaphor may be no more than that and not necessarily a testament to Crabbe's personal experience. Yet given the close interweaving of the content of his poems and his own life, it is easy to imagine that he penned these lines with some knowledge of the metaphor's subject.[21]

---

[17] Crabbe, *Life*, 1947 (1834), p. 138. Cf. Hayter, 1968, p. 165.
[18] Ibid.
[19] Powell, 2004, p. 125.
[20] *The Library*. See Crabbe, *Poetical Works*, 1932, p. 26.
[21] On the autobiographical aspect of Crabbe's poetry, see Powell, 2004, p. 172. Cf. Crabbe's statement, in his 'Autobiographical Sketch' of 1816, that he directly absorbed his own 'knowledge of men and their manners' into his work (Crabbe, 1816, p. 516).

In the second half of 1780, in particular – between the end of his 'Poet's Journal' and his securing of Burke's patronage – Crabbe may well have resorted to the drug. Certainly he seems to have been mentally on the edge when he wrote his first desperate appeal to Burke in February 1781.[22]

The torment of a disturbed mind – and more specifically the spectre of mental illness – were themes to which Crabbe returned many times. *The Library*, in its analogy between violent sea weather and an unstable mind, foreshadows 'Peter Grimes', published some thirty years later: 'Like some vast flood, unbounded, fierce, and strong, / His nature leads ungovern'd man along.'[23] The reality of mental turmoil was certainly something that Crabbe came to experience through his wife's disintegration, in the years after the death of their son Edmund in 1796.

And perhaps Crabbe found in opium a necessary respite from the 'unbounded flood' of his own mind. Neil Powell speculates that he 'attempted to give it up, probably at Sarah's urging, either at around the time of his marriage to her or on moving to Muston'. Conceivably, Powell suggests, the turns Crabbe suffered from – including a spate of dizziness in 1783 while staying with the Elmys in Beccles, and later his attacks of vertigo – were actually symptoms of withdrawal, at moments when he had been unable to obtain a supply. If so, Dr Clubbe's breezy summation of the problem ('let the digestive organs take the blame') could well have been euphemistic – prompted by a recognition of Crabbe's dependency.[24]

But whenever opium began to feature in Crabbe's life, his son's view was that its effects were beneficial – 'to a constant but slightly increasing dose of it may be attributed his long and generally healthy life'.[25] One can well picture Crabbe working, as he did, late at night in his study – with a glass of whisky, laced with a tincture of laudanum.

Later biographers and critics have been less positive. Alethea Hayter, in *Opium and the Romantic Imagination* (1968), concludes that Crabbe, for all his outward appearance of well balanced strength, 'had two of the predisposing characteristics of the potential addict – curiosity about abnormal states of mind and a certain inadequacy in human relationships'.[26] She goes so far as to argue that Crabbe's opium use contributed to a dual intensity of vision and dearth of feeling; that the

---

[22.] Letter to Edmund Burke, February-March 1781. See Crabbe, *Letters*, 1985, p. 5.
[23.] *The Library*. See Crabbe, *Poetical Works*, 1932, p. 31. Cf. Powell, 2004, p. 74.
[24.] Powell, 2004, p. 126.
[25.] Crabbe, *Life*, 1947 (1834), pp. 138–39.
[26.] Hayter, 1968, p. 188. Cf. Powell, 2004, p. 127.

corrupting effect of the drug, 'while it might be revealing to him as a poet, poisoned his relationships with other human beings and impaired his taste by its bias towards violence'.[27]

E.M. Forster also speculated that a recurring unpleasant dream of Crabbe's may have been induced by opium: 'He would dream that he was teased by boys who were made of leather so that when he beat them they felt nothing. "The leather lads have been at me again," he would remark in fatigued tones at the rectory breakfast table.'[28]

There is no evidence that the habit adversely affected the poet's ability to write, but dreams and extreme states of mind did feature increasingly in his writings. A vivid example can be found in *Sir Eustace Grey*, thought to have been started in Crabbe's last years in Suffolk, at Rendham in 1804–05, and published as part of his collected *Poems* in 1807. Sir Eustace is confined to an asylum: he relates to his physician and a visitor the story of his misfortunes and loss of reason. He was once the 'young lord of Greyling Hall', a generous host and the husband of a virtuous wife. But his wife proved faithless and he killed her lover, once his trusted friend, in a duel. She pined and died and their two children quickly followed suit. He recalls how he was tempted by supernatural spirits ('cast from out my state / Two fiends of darkness led my way'), and there follows a phantasmagorical sequence – unfolding across fifteen stanzas – in which he recounts his visions:

> *Those Fiends, upon a shaking Fen,*
> *Fixed me, in dark tempestuous Night;*
> *There never trod the Foot of Men,*
> *There flocked the Fowl in wintry Flight;*
> *There danced the Moor's deceitful Light,*
> *Above the Pool where Sedges grow;*
> *And when the Morning-Sun shone brighter,*
> *It shone upon a Field of Snow.*
>
> *They hung me on a Bough, so small,*
> *The Rook could build her nest no higher;*
> *They fixed me on the trembling Ball,*
> *That crowns the Steeple's quivering Spire;*

[27.] Hayter, 1968, p. 190.
[28.] Forster, 1972 (1948), p. 175; Huchon, 1907, p. 374, n. 5. Cf. the psychoanalytic reading of Hayter, 1968, p. 174: 'The leather lads were disquieting not because they might hurt him, but because he could not hurt them.'

They set me where the Seas retire,
But drown with their returning Tide
And made me flee the Mountain's Fire,
When rolling from its burning Side.

I've hung upon the ridgy Steep
Of Cliffs, and held the rambling Briar;
I've plunged below the billowy Deep,
Where Air was sent me to respire;
I've been where hungry Wolves retire;
And (to complete my Woes) I've ran,
Where Bedlam's crazy Crew conspire
Against the Life of reasoning Man.[29]

The similarity of Sir Eustace's illusions to those described by De Quincey (1785–1859) in his memoir of opium addiction 'is too marked to be accidental', Alfred Ainger writes in his biography. He adds: 'there can be little doubt that Crabbe's poem owes its inception to opium and that the framework was devised by him for the utilisation of his dreams.'[30]

Again, after Crabbe's death a copy of verses, undated and entitled *The World of Dreams,* was found among his many manuscript notebooks. Unlike any other narrative poem of Crabbe's apart from the fragmentary *Where Am I Now?* of 1819–22, it is written in the first person in his own character.[31] The verses are in the same metre and rhyme scheme as *Sir Eustace Grey,* and deal in the same kind of visions as recorded by the inmate of the asylum. 'The rapid and continuous transition from scene to scene, and period to period, is the same in both,' Ainger contends. 'Foreign kings and other potentates reappear, as with De Quincey, in ghostly and repellent forms.'

Ainger also draws a comparison between Crabbe's poem, below, and Coleridge's 'The Pains of Sleep' (written in 1803), adding: 'It can hardly be doubted that the two poems had a common origin'.[32]

[29.] *Sir Eustace Grey*, 172–73, 268–91. See Crabbe, *Poems*, 2015, p. 37, p. 40.
[30.] Ainger, 1903, p. 85. Cf. Hayter, 1968, p. 170: 'this [story] expressed not what he had observed in others, but what he had felt in himself.'
[31.] Hayter, 1968, p. 179.
[32.] Ainger, 1903, p. 89.

> *I know not how, but I am brought*
> *Into a large and Gothic hall,*
> *Seated with those I never sought –*
> *Kings, Caliphs, Kaisers – silent all;*
> *Pale as the dead; enrobed and tall,*
> *Majestic, frozen, solemn, still;*
> *They wake my fears, my wits appal,*
> *And with both scorn and terror fill.*[33]

These fantastic imaginings are a far cry from the earthy realism of much of Crabbe's work. But although the year of *Sir Eustace Grey*, about 1805, was a time of poetic renaissance generally, Crabbe was not tempted to 'tread the fresh woods and pastures new that were opening before him'. He never faltered, writes Ainger, in the conviction that his own strength lay elsewhere: 'not in the romantic or the mystical – not in perfection of form or melody of lyric verse, were his own humbler triumphs to be won'.

'Like Wordsworth,' Ainger adds, 'he was to find a sufficiency in the "common growth of mother-earth", though indeed less in her "mirth" than in her "tears".'[34]

Crabbe and Politics:
We can do no good, or we would be among them

At the far end of Aldeburgh Beach, overlooking the North Sea on one side and the Alde estuary on the other, is a squat, quatrefoil-shaped stone tower. Sited at the point where the shingle beach starts to recede into the stark wastes of the Orford peninsula, it is a local landmark – visible for miles across the expanse of marshes that lie inland.

The Martello Tower, one of nine such buildings surviving in Britain – and the largest – was built as a defence against Napoleon. It stands next to where Slaughden Quay was once a bustling port, and where Crabbe worked for his father, the Saltmaster.

The tower is the most northerly of a chain of defensive fortifications built along the south-eastern coastlines of England in the early nineteenth century, in response to the threat of invasion by France. When they were

---

[33] *The World of Dreams*, XXVIII. See Crabbe, *Poetical Works*, 1932, p. 585.
[34] Ainger, 1903, p. 89.

constructed, the towers were known as heavy gun batteries, but acquired the name Martello from the tower that had provided the inspiration for their design. This stood on Mortella Point in Corsica.

The tower was built between 1808 and 1812 – in Crabbe's lifetime; he is likely to have seen it on return visits to Aldeburgh. But in 1805, when the family visited to bid the town *adieu* before returning to Muston, it was not yet in existence. In these years, the 'dread of a French invasion was at its height', as Crabbe's son recalls, and the town possessed a large calibre cannon that was 'constantly primed, as an alarm gun'.[35]

It was during this trip, at around one o'clock one night, that the younger George Crabbe heard distant gunfire at sea and then 'the tremendous roar of the great gun on the fort, which shook every house in town'. George knocked on his father's door with the news that the French were landing: the alarm gun had been fired and horsemen dispatched for troops stationed at Ipswich. Crabbe was philosophical to the point of insouciance, remarking: 'Well, my old fellow, you and I can do no good, or we would be among them.' When his son returned in three quarters of an hour to tell his father that the 'agitation was subsiding', he found him fast asleep. 'I remember that my father's coolness on the occasion, when we mentioned it next day, caused some suspicious shaking of the head among the ultraloyalists of Aldborough.'[36]

He lived in a time of great social and political upheaval – the movement towards franchise reform, the Gordon Riots of 1780 (several days of rioting in London that started as an anti-Catholic protest that he personally witnessed), the French Revolution, and then the Napoleonic Wars and the American War of Independence. And all the while, the Industrial Revolution was grinding into life.

But he had no strong party political allegiances, and – as his poetry reflects – seems to have been more of a dispassionate observer than an idealist or an agitator in political matters.

Before Crabbe had returned to Muston following his thirteen-year sojourn in Suffolk, however, there were rumours circulating that he was a Jacobin – sympathetic to the French revolutionaries.

> By degrees, the tale [...] gained a pretty general credence among a population, which being purely agricultural – and therefore, connecting every notion of what was praiseworthy with the maintenance of the war that, undoubtedly, had

---

[35] Crabbe, *Life*, 1947 (1834), p. 153.
[36] Ibid.

raised agricultural prices to an unprecedented scale – was affected in a manner extremely disagreeable to my father's feelings, and even worldly interests, by such an impression as thus originated.[37]

Not for the first time, Crabbe was exposed to the disdain of sections of the Aldeburgh community – this time for his seeming failure to share their bellicose spirit in the face of the French Revolutionary Wars. The charge of his being a sympathiser even found its way up to Muston ahead of him, ensuring a frosty reception when he arrived.

The reality, his son asserts, was otherwise:

> The truth is, that my father never was a politician – that is to say, he never allowed political affairs to occupy much of his mind at any period of his life, or thought either better or worse of any individual for the bias he had received. But he did not, certainly, approve of the *origin* of the war that was raging while he lived at Parham, Glemham, and Rendham; nor did he ever conceal his opinion, that this war might have been avoided – and hence, in proportion to the weight of his local character, he gave offence to persons maintaining the diametrically opposite view of public matters at that particular crisis.

'As to the term *Jacobin*,' adds Crabbe's son in a flash of filial loyalty, 'I shall say only one word. None could have been less fitly applied to him at any period of his life [...] No syllable in approbation of Jacobins or Jacobinism ever came from his tongue or from his pen.'

Circumspect and accommodating, Crabbe was no stranger to the society of politicians of various hues. In his early years especially, he inclined towards liberals and liberalism; like Wordsworth and many others of their generation, he had some sympathy with the French revolutionaries' ideals at the outset – even if he decried the way that the revolution developed. This marked him out as an anomaly in the household of the Duke of Rutland, when he became chaplain in 1782. 'At Belvoir he had more than once to drink a glass of salt water, because he would not join in Tory toasts', his son records. 'He preserved his

---

[37] Ibid, p. 149.

early partialities through all his trying time of Tory patronage; and of course he felt, on the whole, a greater political accord with the owner of Glemham and his distinguished guests.'[38]

As a young man, certainly, Crabbe kept the company of the leading Whigs of the day. Little Glemham Hall, the home of Dudley North, was where he met public figures such as Charles James Fox and Charles (Earl) Grey – who would later, as Prime Minister, oversee the Reform Act of 1832 and the Slavery Abolition Act of 1833.[39] Crabbe had mixed with such figures since his first acquaintanceship with Edmund Burke, his great patron. Burke was a prominent Whig at the time they met in 1781, although he later became estranged from the party.

Crabbe's son believes that Crabbe offered Burke the dedication of *The Newspaper* in 1785, and possibly some of his earlier works – *The Library* in 1781 and *The Village* in 1783. But 'that great man, probably from modesty, declined anything of this kind'.[40]

Since dedications were the only way Crabbe could repay Burke's kindness and generosity, he became increasingly reluctant to raise the subject of poetry with Burke – and their correspondence diminished and finally ceased. Burke died in 1797.

Some commentators have seen the lack of correspondence in the last dozen years of Burke's life as signifying a lack of gratitude on Crabbe's part. But there is a simpler and more likely explanation – that Burke had removed himself from public life, and with it, the prolific discourse of earlier times. In his later years, Burke became increasingly alienated from politics, except for his prominent role in the trial of Warren Hastings between 1887 and 1895.[41] Crabbe, immersed in family life in these years, had himself withdrawn from political society and ceased to publish. During his twenty-two-year hiatus, he may have felt that Burke expected him to publish more – another potential reason for the lapse in communication.[42]

[38.] Ibid, p. 150.

[39.] Crabbe, *Life*, 1947 (1834), p. 133. Cf. Powell, 2004, p. 141.

[40.] Crabbe, *Life*, 1947 (1834), p. 115.

[41.] See Crabbe, *Letters*, 1985, p. 391: Appendix. Hastings, the first and most famous of the British governors general of India, dominated Indian affairs from 1772 to 1785. He was impeached by the House of Commons – with Burke leading the prosecution – between 1887 and 1895, accused of misconduct, mismanagement, personal corruption and maltreatment of the natives – but was acquitted.

[42.] Ibid.

Crabbe was writing, nonetheless, at a time of upheaval: whatever his personal affiliations, the epoch brought its own inescapable backdrop in the shape of the Industrial Revolution. When at Belvoir, he met with Dr Edmund Cartwright, rector of Goadby Marwood, a neighbouring parish to Stathern, and later Prebendary of Lincoln – but also a poet. Cartwright constructed a prototype of the power loom which he patented in 1785, before setting up a factory in Doncaster to put it into practice along with his wool-combing machine, developed in 1790. Crabbe visited the factory with his wife, but according to their son, the occasion proved more traumatic than edifying: when Sarah 'entered the vast building, full of engines thundering with resistless power, yet under the apparent management of children, the bare idea of the inevitable hazard attendant on such stupendous undertakings, quite overcame her feelings, and she burst into tears'.[43] (Crabbe also became friends with Cartwright's son, also Edmund, who was twenty years his junior – and, like Crabbe, a keen botanist.)

Over the years, Crabbe's politics appear to have grown more conservative, although the shift was undoubtedly gentler than Wordsworth's transformation from a youthful radical to a hard-line reactionary. But that, argues his son, was in line with the tendency of every young man 'to adopt what are called popular or liberal opinions' before he raises himself to some more elevated station in the world, at which point he is apt to 'imbibe aristocratic sentiments [...] Such is, probably, the natural tendency of such a rise in society.'[44]

The younger Crabbe elaborates:

> He became still more intimate with the highest ranks of society, and mingled with them [...] as one whom talent had placed above the suspicion of subserviency; when he felt the full advantages of his rise, and became the rector of a large town, and a magistrate, I think again, the aristocratic and Tory leanings he then showed were rather the effect of these circumstances than of any alteration of judgment founded upon deliberate inquiry and reflection.[45]

---

[43] Crabbe, *Life*, 1947 (1834), pp. 117–18.
[44] Ibid, p. 150.
[45] Ibid, p. 151.

Throughout his life, Crabbe remained indifferent to party politics, variously dedicating his books to those of opposite opinion and lending his support on occasion to candidates from both Whig and Tory parties.

Perhaps, then, he was a conservative by circumstance rather than deep conviction. Tellingly, he was not opposed to electoral reform: writing in his last full year, 1831 – the year before the Reform Act was enacted – he remarked:

> I believe there is a fund of good sense as well as moral feeling in the people of this country; and if ministers proceed steadily, give up some points and be firm in essentials, there will be a union of sentiment on this great subject of reform by and by; at least, the good and well-meaning will drop their minor differences and be united.[46]

Where Crabbe had political passion it was not for any party or ideology so much as for the plight of the poor – as he vividly and dispassionately expressed in his writings. In this, he went against the romanticism and pastoral idealism of many contemporaries, determined to expose the lot of the disadvantaged and downtrodden as he saw it – and painting what he called 'the real picture of the poor'.[47]

> *I paint the cot,*
> *As truth will paint it, and as bards will not.*[48]

[46.] Crabbe, *Life*, 1947 (1834), p. 275.
[47.] *The Village*, Book I, 6. See Crabbe, *Poems*, 2015, p. 5.
[48.] *The Village*, Book I, 54–55: ibid, p. 6.

Chapter 5

Character and Creation

Aldeburgh: I hear those voices that will not be drowned

Turn northwards on Aldeburgh beach towards Thorpeness, and you soon spot a sliver of metallic light arising from the beach. It grows in dimensions on approach, broadening to assume the form of a huge multifaceted scallop shell. 'I hear those voices that will not be drowned' is inscribed in the glinting steel of the sculpture.

Maggi Hambling's iconic *Scallop* (2003) is a striking and powerful tribute to Benjamin Britten. The words cut into its upper extremity, across the fluted metal, come from his opera *Peter Grimes* (1945): they are the most forceful evocation in Aldeburgh of the composer.

Yet the inscription and sculpture also serve to recall Crabbe and his most famous work. For it was Crabbe who first depicted the reclusive fisherman of Aldeburgh and the brutal deeds that haunted him to his death. The story comes in the twelfth 'Letter' of Crabbe's twenty-four-part collection *The Borough* (1810), a depiction of the inhabitants and life of a fictional community – and it was this which the poet Montagu Slater adapted to form the libretto for Britten's opera.

The line of text in Hambling's sculpture is not Crabbe's: it is drawn from a monologue by Grimes in the libretto, and refers to those 'dead figures', revenants from the past, who haunt the fisherman and dispel his fantasies of a happier, kinder existence.[1]

[1.] Compare the lines spoken by Grimes on his deathbed, as he describes the ghostly visitations he has experienced (see over):

Perhaps, though, the phrase can also be seen as a metaphor for the artistic voices that have been drawn over the centuries to the setting of Aldeburgh – not least Hambling. Like Crabbe, Britten and many others, Hambling was inspired by the place – the landscape and seascape – or what E.M. Forster memorably called 'the sea, the estuary, the flat Suffolk coast, and local meanness, and an odour of brine and dirt – tempered occasionally with the scent of flowers'.[2]

'I wanted it to be very much a sea piece – in much the same way as Britten's "Sea Interludes" are', Hambling has explained:

> *Scallop* is subtitled *A Conversation with the Sea*. So it had, of course, to be on the shingle, close to the sea. The sculpture stands on the stretch of beach that Britten walked and where I'm told he swam every day of the year. And I wanted to provide a place of contemplation where someone, whatever his or her state of mind, would be invited to contemplate the sea, the horizon, to think, as most people do when they look at the sea, about time and life and death.[3]

She also wished to reflect the way in which Britten had 'smashed classical music and remade it in his own voice', by creating an equivalent disruption. 'I wanted a strangeness, like the unlikely juxtapositions of Britten's music, something come upon unexpectedly as one drove along the road between Aldeburgh and Thorpeness.'[4]

That strange and unexpected quality may account for the hostility felt by some of the Aldeburgh townspeople when *Scallop* was first erected – although the sculpture has since become a loved and admired landmark. Aldeburgh, like any town, has always had its reactionary elements; Crabbe knew this better than anyone. Hambling's eagerness to create a

---

> And "Come," they said, with weak, sad voices, "come."
> To row away with all my strength I tried,
> But there were they, hard by me in the Tide,
> The three unbodied Forms – and "Come", they said, still "come"
>   they cried.
> Crabbe, Poems, 2015, p. 92.

[2.] Forster, 1941, p. 769. See Chapter 1.
[3.] Maggi Hambling, *The Aldeburgh Scallop* (Framlingham: Full Circle Editions, 2010), p. 20.
[4.] Ibid.

Figure 15. Maggi Hambling, *Scallop*, 2013

Figure 16. Peter Grimes on Aldeburgh Beach, first-night performance, 17 June 2013

monument to Britten had been prompted, in part, by an earlier decision of the town council to decline an offer to erect a statue in the composer's honour: they wanted to use the funds instead to build a bird bath or plant trees.[5]

The reluctance to commemorate Britten properly has prompted allegations of lurking homophobia. Perhaps at the very least it can be seen as a sign of conservative resistance towards the town's artistic milieu. But it is worth remembering that the town did take Britten and Pears to its heart, from the 1940s through to the 70s – during most of which time homosexuality was illegal – or at least was happy to turn a blind eye.

In defying Aldeburgh's one-time resistance, Hambling created a work that belongs to the people, inviting individual engagement. She has stressed the personal dimension of the sculpture. 'People are encouraged to contemplate the horizon and the movement of the waves, and to have a conversation not only with the sea but also with themselves. To listen to their own voices.'[6]

There are parallels between Crabbe, Britten and Hambling. For Hambling, as with Britten and Crabbe, the coastline is imbued with memories of childhood: 'In my slow Suffolk way I realised many years later that the seed of *Scallop* was sown inside me when I was seven, watching fireworks exploding over the sea at Aldeburgh for the Coronation, or even earlier – as a toddler taking to the waves.'[7]

Crabbe, too, drew on his time as a child and young adult in Suffolk in writing *The Borough*. The settings of the twenty-four tales or Letters embrace other places, drawing upon the various parishes in which he had spent time as a clergyman, but as he wrote to his friend Elizabeth Charter in 1824, Aldeburgh was the 'Suffolk-Borough which helped me to my Scenery & some of my Characters in the Poem which I have called by that Name'.[8] And as Powell observes of 'Peter Grimes' in particular, 'although Crabbe's *Borough* is a fictional and composite place, this poem is plainly set in the childhood landscape and seascape, briefly invoked in

---

[5.] See John Vidal, 'The rise and fall of the statue', *The Guardian*, 27 July 1996.
[6.] Ibid, p. 21.
[7.] Ibid.
[8.] Letter to Elizabeth Charter, 9 November 1824. See Crabbe, *Letters*, 1985, p. 308. Cf. Ainger, 1903, p. 109: '*The Borough* is Aldeburgh extended and magnified.'

"The Parish-Clerk" and "Abel Keene" [Letters XIX and XXI of the poem], which would subsequently reappear in the powerfully autobiographical "Infancy – a Fragment".[9]

* * *

The tale of Peter Grimes is, of course, the most famous of the stories in *The Borough*. Its main character was utterly compromised, morally. From where did such a character originate? According to Crabbe's son in a footnote to the 1834 edition of *The Poetical Works of the Rev. George Crabbe*, Grimes was based on an old fisherman of Aldeburgh at the time Crabbe was there as a surgeon-apothecary:

> He had a succession of apprentices from London, and a certain sum from each. As the boys disappeared under circumstances of strong suspicion, the man was warned by some of the principal inhabitants, that if another followed in like manner he would certainly be charged with murder.[10]

In the latter part of Crabbe's poem, Grimes descends into madness, is tormented with visions, and dies, haunted by the ghosts of the children he has murdered. Later, in a manuscript annotation on the same page, Crabbe's son identified the man: 'Tom Brown. The death of the apprentices was most suspicious. The Terrors imaginary, I believe.'[11] Others point out that the character's story also draws on the case of John Bennett, a fisherman living in Hammersmith, west London, who was indicted for the murder of an apprentice who had died, like Grimes's second apprentice, by falling from a mast.[12]

But did Crabbe also draw elements of the character from his own father, and from their difficult relationship? The poem begins with Grimes defying, scorning and coming to blows with his aged father, before taking to drink when the old man dies. Grimes speaks later of 'My father's spirit – he who always tried / To give me trouble, when he lived and died' (see Chapter 2), and it is hard not to make a connection between that bitter reflection and Crabbe's own fractious paternal

---

[9.] Powell, 2004, p. 191.
[10.] *The Poetical Works of the Rev. George Crabbe: with his Letters and Journals, and his Life, by his Son*, Vol. IV (London: John Murray, 1834), p. 90, n. 1. Cf. Whitehead, 1995, p. 82.
[11.] Ibid. Cf. Huchon, 1907, p. 310, n. 1.
[12.] Whitehead, 1995, p. 83.

bond.[13] Crabbe fell out with his father after the death of his mother, when the former remarried, but the relationship had never been an easy one. By the end, his father had turned to drink, becoming increasingly erratic and given to violent outbursts of a kind to which Grimes himself succumbs.

Grimes feels himself to be haunted not only by the ghosts of the dead boys, but also the malign spirit of the father he spurned. Yet for all Grimes's aberrations, Crabbe retains a certain sympathy with his character. Grimes, as Powell argues, 'is possessed of forces which are both destructive and self-destructive', and ultimately, 'in a crucial sense he is not to blame' – or not solely – because the townsfolk stand by and do nothing about his cruel behaviour and the beatings he inflicted – remarking calmly: '*Grimes* is at his Exercise.'[14] This note of guarded sympathy resonates, again, with the ambivalence Crabbe felt about his own father – an antipathy edged with compassion.

The Borough was published in February 1810, after Crabbe left Suffolk. But he had started writing it during his four years at Rendham from 1801. He continued the collection when he left Suffolk for Muston in 1805, finally completing it on a long visit to Aldeburgh in 1809. Friends of the Crabbes at Aldeburgh had invited them 'to taste the sea air after four years' residence in the centre of the kingdom'. This they did – and Crabbe brought with him his manuscript for completion, to be inspected by his friend at Great Yarmouth – the Rev. Richard Turner – 'without whose council [sic] he decided on nothing'.[15] In all, the 10,000 or so lines had been eight years in the making.[16]

The work went through six editions in six years. It was a success from the outset. Its honest and grim picture of life in a country town would later prompt Alfred Ainger to remark: 'it even reminds us of a saying of Tennyson's, that if god made the country, and man made the city, then it was the devil who made the country-town'.[17]

There was also a degree of shock, when the poem first appeared, at its blunt, unrestrained *exposé* of humankind's vices. Writing in *The Edinburgh Review* in April 1810, the critic Francis Jeffrey commented

---

[13.] 'Peter Grimes', Letter XXII, *The Borough*, 291–92. See Crabbe, *Poems*, 2015, p. 91. On the links between Grimes and Crabbe's father, see Powell, 2004, pp. 193–95.

[14.] Powell, 2004, p. 195. Crabbe, *Poems,* 2015, p. 85, line 78.

[15.] Crabbe, *Life,* 1947 (1834), p. 168.

[16.] Ainger, 1903, p. 109.

[17.] Ibid, p. 118.

that Crabbe's 'chief fault [...] is his frequent lapse into disgusting representations; and this, we will confess, is an error for which we find it far more difficult either to account or to apologise' – more, that is, than the poet's habit of 'drawing characters, for no other purpose, but to indulge his taste, and to display his talents'.

Jeffrey added: 'On the characters, miseries and vices of such beings, we look with *disgust* merely', though he conceded that they may occasionally 'serve some moral purpose. [...] we turn away from them, therefore, with loathing and dispassionate aversion; – we feel our imaginations polluted by the intrusion of any images connected with them; and are offended and disgusted when we are forced to look closely upon those festering heaps of moral filth and corruption.'

It was a devastating critique. For good measure, Jeffrey concluded that 'no writer has sinned so deeply in this respect as Mr Crabbe – who has so often presented us with spectacles which it is purely painful and degrading to contemplate'.[18]

Jeffrey was not alone, even if his jeremiad was more blistering than most. As the critic Jerome McGann has noted, 'people like Wordsworth, Coleridge, Hazlitt [...] found the work repellent. Their legacy is to be traced not so much in a body of negative criticism as in the absence of any criticism at all.'[19] Wordsworth took a disapproving view in general of Crabbe's use of everyday 'matters of fact' out of the newspapers as the stuff of poetry, resulting in poems with which 'the Muses have just about as much to do as they have with a Collection of medical reports, or of Law Cases'.[20]

Various other readers of *The Borough* also found Crabbe's realist view of humanity distasteful: one anonymous writer in *The Monthly Mirror* of August 1810 noted – somewhat inaccurately, and disregarding the inland places where the poet had lived – that 'Mr Crabbe has lived a great deal in a smuggling neighbourhood, and has observed that the country there is a very different thing from what our Arcadian poets have represented it: he therefore very naturally falls into the other extreme, and sees nothing but vice in every village and poverty in every

---

[18.] Francis Jeffrey, unsigned review in *The Edinburgh Review*, Vol. 16 (April 1810): p. 38.

[19.] Jerome McGann, 'George Crabbe: Poetry and Truth', *London Review of Books*, Vol. 11, No. 6 (16 March 1989): p. 16.

[20.] Quoted in Markham L. Peacock, *The Critical Opinions of William Wordsworth* (Baltimore: Johns Hopkins University Press, 1950), p. 235.

cottage.'[21] In the opinion of this reviewer, the character of Grimes was too debased even to act as an exemplar of immorality: 'The story of Peter Grimes [...] is either completely out of nature, or ought no more to be drawn for the determent of man, than a Portsmouth trull for a warning to the fair sex.'[22]

Crabbe himself had written a preface to *The Borough*, an exposition and defence of his subject in which he anticipated that his poem would prove offensive 'to those of extremely delicate feelings'.[23] This only served to arouse further the annoyance of some reviewers, who saw it as a self-justifying apology for his work. The outraged critic of *The Monthly Mirror* accused Crabbe of usurping his own role: 'it looks more like a favourable review, than any thing else. We, as reviewers, must protest against this invasion of our province: we are put out of our bread, if every author is thus to become his own reviewer.'[24]

The poet James Montgomery, writing in *The Eclectic Review* in June, fulminated: 'This preface is a tissue of explanations and apologies to the extent of nearly *thirty pages;* and is altogether most singularly tiresome, unnecessary, and injudicious.' Yet Montgomery did also acknowledge, 'for energy of conception and effect', what he called the book's masterpiece: the story of Peter Grimes. 'We have been particularly struck,' he wrote, 'with the peculiar and unrivalled skill, with which Mr Crabbe paints the horrors of a disordered imagination; a pre-eminence which we can only account for, by supposing it may have been his mournful privilege, for a considerable length of time, to watch the emotions and hear the ravings of the insane.'[25] (That latter supposition had validity: Crabbe's long experience of his wife's illness – let alone his other experiences – must surely have filtered into his portrayals of disturbed minds.) And many leading reviewers agreed that *The Borough* had at once greater beauties and greater defects than its predecessor, *The Parish Register*.[26]

[21.] Unsigned review in *The Monthly Mirror*, Vols. 7 and 8 (August and October 1810): pp. 126–34, 280–84, p. 281. Quoted in Powell, 2004, p. 201.

[22.] Ibid.

[23.] 'Preface', *The Borough*. See *Poetical Works*, 1932, p. 101.

[24.] Unsigned review in *The Monthly Mirror*, Vol. 7 (August 1810), p. 127. Quoted in Powell, 2004, p. 202.

[25.] James Montgomery, unsigned review in *The Eclectic Review*, Vol. 6 (June 1810): pp. 546–61. Cf. Powell, 2004, pp. 202–203.

[26.] Crabbe, *Life*, 1947 (1834), p. 169.

The voices of disapproval that choroused in response to *The Borough*, like the voices that condemned Maggi Hambling's *Scallop* when it first appeared on the coast, have drowned in obscurity. What remains is the precision and power with which Crabbe intertwined character and landscape, probing the depths of human behaviour.

And disgust aside, many contemporary readers did appreciate these aspects, as Ainger would in the following century, and Britten after him: 'To travel through the borough from end to end is to pass through much ignoble scenery, human and other, and under a cloudy heaven, with only rare gleams of sunshine, and patches of blue sky,' Ainger wrote. 'These, when they occur, are proportionately welcome. They include some exquisite descriptions of nature, though with Crabbe it will be noticed that it is always the nature close about his feet, the hedge-row the meadow, the cottage-garden: as his son has noted, his outlook never extends to the landscape beyond.'[27]

Aldeburgh: Grimes on the beach

The night was cool but buzzing with anticipation. In June 2013, an epic production of the opera *Peter Grimes* was staged over three nights on Aldeburgh beach. Ambitious and spectacular, it was a perfect way to mark the centenary of Benjamin Britten's birth. The audience camped largely on the shingle beach, although there were some raised seats, and watched the opera play out on the same shoreline that Britten frequently trod (as captured by the photographer Hans Wild in 1959), and in the very setting of Crabbe's original story, written two hundred years earlier. With fortuitous timing, the sky was lowering with clouds as a Spitfire soared overhead, performing a victory roll by way of an overture to the first orchestral interlude.

The dramatic fly-by signalled the shifting of the story, by director Tim Albery and designer Leslie Travers, from the early nineteenth century of Crabbe's poem to the 1940s – the same decade in which Britten settled in Suffolk and composed *Peter Grimes*. But the evocation of the town transcended any specific period – consisting of a scaffold of raked wooden platforms and scattered fishing boats, oil drums and lookout towers silhouetted against the evening sky. The scenery – like the

---

[27.] Ainger, 1903, p. 118.

surrounding beach – reflected the layers of time and memory that are characteristic of Aldeburgh. As the cast began the first of their rousing, ominous choruses, a spray of rain swept across the beach.

'A stiff breeze whistles down the Suffolk coast from Sizewell', was how the critic of *The Times*, Richard Morrison, described the experience:

> Behind the stage, whipped-up waves crash on shingle. As midnight approaches mist drifts in from the sea. And, as the thermometer dips and we sink deeper into our thermals, so the temperature of the drama rises. […] On the beach at Aldeburgh, where he once hauled in his fishing nets, Peter Grimes has come home […] Here is a borough with primeval bloodlust lurking just beneath the social veneer.[28]

Other critics were similarly spellbound by the staging and performances. 'It's a wonderfully potent setting for an opera whose every bar is permeated by the sea,' wrote Andrew Clements in *The Guardian*:

> Some elements in the story – Balstrode and Ned Keene helping Grimes land his boat in the first act, the villagers setting off to march to Grimes's hut in the second; Grimes setting off from the beach for the final time – acquire an extra layer of realism in such a visual context.[29]

The performance was long – close to four hours – and sitting on the shingle uncomfortable, with the cold and damp kept at bay by waterproof jackets and flasks of spirits and wine. But it was unforgettable – a brilliant fusion of the story of Grimes, Britten's haunting music, and Aldeburgh itself in different moments: the present tense of 2013, the mid-century era of Britten's first arrival in the town, and the 'little venal borough' of Crabbe's day. Beyond the temporary edifice of the stage, of course, stretched the ever-present and constant expanse of the sea.

Britten's creation was inspired, like Crabbe's before him, by this place. The composer wrote of the power and symbolism of the sea in the preface to the first performance of *Peter Grimes* at Sadler's Wells in 1945:

[28.] Richard Morrison, 'Peter Grimes at Aldeburgh Beach, Suffolk', *The Times*, 19 June 2013.

[29.] Andrew Clements, 'Grimes on the Beach – Review', *The Guardian*, 18 June 2013.

Character and Creation

> For most of my life I have lived closely in touch with the sea. My parent's [sic] house in Lowestoft directly faced the sea, and my life as a child was coloured by the fierce storms that sometimes drove ships on to our coast and ate away whole stretches of the neighbouring cliffs.

He went on to suggest a metaphoric connection between the sea – a temperamental force, mutable and elemental – and the musical form of his opera, in which the emotional register continually shifts and fluctuates:

> In writing *Peter Grimes*, I wanted to express my awareness of the perpetual struggle of men and women whose livelihood depends on the sea – difficult though it is to treat such a universal subject in theatrical form. I am especially interested in the general architectural and formal problems of opera, and decided to reject the Wagnerian theory of 'permanent melody' for the classical practice of separate numbers that crystallize and hold the emotion of a dramatic situation at chosen moments.
>   One of my chief aims is to try and restore to the musical setting of the English language a brilliance, freedom and vitality that have been curiously rare since the death of Purcell. In the past hundred years, English writing for the voice has been dominated by strict subservience to logical speech-rhythms, despite the fact that accentuation according to sense often contradicts the accentuation demanded by emotional content. Good recitative should transform the natural intonations and rhythms of everyday speech into memorable musical phrases (as with Purcell), but in more stylized music, the composer should not deliberately avoid unnatural stresses if the prosody of the poem and the emotional situation demand them, nor be afraid of a highhanded treatment of words, which may need prolongation far beyond their common speech length, or a speed of delivery that would be impossible in conversation.[30]

The emotional tension in *Peter Grimes* mounts and darkens as the outcast fisherman disappears, and the widow Mrs Sedley whips up a mob to track him down ('Him who despises us we'll destroy'). Grimes

---

[30.] Britten, 1945, pp. 7–8.

appears and sings a monologue that lays bare his maddened state. He is discovered by Ellen, a schoolmistress, and the retired merchantman Balstrode, who persuades him to take his boat out to sea and sink himself.

On Aldeburgh beach, the finale played out amid a downpour as the clouds finally erupted. One wanted Britten to be there to take a bow. But, of course, also George Crabbe, the source of this strange and haunting story of crime, punishment and insanity on the Suffolk shores. To repeat Forster, 'Crabbe without Aldeburgh, Peter Grimes without the estuary of the Alde, would lose their savour and tang.'[31] He might easily have added Britten to the mix. They are all intertwined.[32]

Aldeburgh: *Untouched by pity, unstung by remorse*

For the character of Peter Grimes, Britten drew on Crabbe – but the two men's conceptions were different. Crabbe, in his preface to *The Borough*, sought to explain the character of his brutal fisherman:

> The mind here exhibited is one untouched by pity, unstung by remorse and uncorrected by shame: yet is this hardihood of temper and spirit broken by want, disease, solitude, and disappointment; and he becomes the victim of a distempered and horror-stricken fancy. It is evident, therefore, that no feeble vision, no half-visible ghost, not the momentary glance of an unbodied being, nor the half-audible voice of an invisible one, would be created by the continual workings of distress on a mind so deprived and flinty.[33]

In rationalising the extremes of both Grimes's depravity and torment, Crabbe also betrayed a certain guarded empathy for Grimes as victim of wretched circumstances:

> The corrosion of hapless want, the wasting of unabating disease, and the gloom of unvaried solitude, will have their effect on every nature; and the harder that nature is, and

---

[31.] Forster, 1972 (1948), p 167.

[32.] Blake Morrison, 'The Man Behind Manjamin Britten', *The Guardian*, 14 June 2013.

[33.] 'Preface', *The Borough*. See *Poetical Works*, 1932, pp. 106–107.

the longer time required to work upon it, so much the more strong and indelible is the impression.

'This is all the reason I am able to give,' he concluded, 'why a man of feeling so dull should yet became insane, [and why the visions of his distempered brain] should be of so horrible a nature.'[34]

In Britten's opera – first performed at Sadler's Wells, London, on 7 June 1945 with Peter Pears in the title role – Grimes is a more explicitly sympathetic character. He is still an outsider, as with Crabbe, but no longer an unqualified villain – more a tortured idealist. As one critic has put it:

> A man of passion and intelligence, with a strong desire to succeed as a fisherman; a man who wants to marry the schoolmistress, the widow Mrs Ellen Orford, settle down and become respectable; a man at hopeless odds with the community who is more sinned against than sinning. He is, in short, a sanitised version of the Grimes depicted by Crabbe in 1810.[35]

The injured idealism of the man who feels himself thwarted by his community is conveyed in Montagu Slater's libretto; in anguish, Grimes demands of Ellen Orford:

> *Wrong to plan?*
> *Wrong to try?*
> *Wrong to live?*
> *Right to die?*
> *Wrong to struggle?*
> *Wrong to hope?*
> *Then the Borough's Right again?*[36]

In both poem and opera, there is the malign power of gossip: Peter Grimes is hounded by the 'Borough', a mix of town officials and

---

[34.] Ibid. The words in parenthesis are omitted from this edition but appear in others.
[35.] Tom Rosenthal, 'Who was the real Peter Grimes?', *The Independent*, 17 July 2013.
[36.] Montagu Slater, libretto for *Peter Grimes*, 1945. See Benjamin Britten, Montagu Slater, *Peter Grimes: An Opera in Three Acts and a Prologue* (London: Boosey & Hawkes, 1961), p. 29.

gossiping townsfolk. In the opera, Ellen tells him: 'You'll never stop the gossips talk [...] We were mistaken to have dreamed.'[37] As the Reverend Canon Nigel Hartley (vicar of Aldeburgh from 2004 to 2014) has remarked: 'some see a semi-autobiographical portrait of Britten as an outsider to the society of his day because of his relationship with Peter Pears. Alan Britten, Benjamin Britten's nephew and a member of our congregation, says that Britten told him that his portrait was of the destructive power of the borough gossips and nothing else.'[38] The production of Grimes on the beach in the centenary year of Britten's birth brought the Aldeburgh gossips vividly to life and, Hartley adds, 'more than one person commented that Crabbe and Britten might still feel their portraits to be accurate!'[39]

The Grimes of Crabbe's *Borough* takes in a young boy as an apprentice, brutally and sadistically ill-treating him (in the opera, Grimes's ill-intent is less explicit). The boy dies, as do two more apprentices in the fisherman's care. The townsfolk fail to intervene, turning a blind eye: 'None inquired how Peter used the rope, / Or what the bruise, that made the stripling stoop.' Finally after the suspicious deaths of the three boys, Grimes is barred by the parish authorities from taking any more apprentices.

From this time, Grimes is hounded by a hostile community, haunted by the ghosts of his father and the three dead boys. He descends into madness, dying in the poorhouse. He becomes a recluse amid the marshes and their brackish waters. The scene prefigures Forster's evocation of a bleak and brine-drenched wilderness, except here there is no redeeming scent of flowers. Cast out by the townsfolk, Grimes is

> *by himself compelled to live each day,*
> *To wait for certain hours the Tide's delay;*
> *At the same times the same dull views to see,*
> *The bounding Marsh-bank and the blighted Tree;*
> *The Water only, when the Tides were high,*
> *When low, the Mud half-covered and half-dry;*
> *The Sun-Burnt Tar that blisters on the Planks,*
> *And Bank-side Stakes in their uneven ranks;*

---

[37] Ibid.
[38] Hartley, 2014, p. 5. Alan Britten died in 2016.
[39] Ibid.

Heaps of entangled Weeds that slowly float,
As the Tide Rolls by the impeded Boat.[40]

This landscape is much more than a geographical backdrop. It becomes Grimes's own personal hell, a place of moral reckoning. Crabbe, as Edmund Blunden has noted, was, after all, concerned with the state of mind of individuals, the psychological landscape, and the effect of mood on the appearance of nature.[41] In the simpler, blunter lines of Slater's libretto, Grimes makes it equally clear that he is steeped in his native place; asked why he doesn't venture further afield, he replies that he is rooted

By familiar fields,
Marsh and sand,
Ordinary streets,
Prevailing wind.[42]

It is unsurprising that Britten and Pears were seized by the story. If Peter Grimes, through Britten, has become the most famous of Crabbe's portrayals, one reason is the power of the poet's lines – among his most evocative and compelling. Despite Forster's rather harsh view that they are 'not great poetry' (see Chapter 1), they are the most rooted in the land and seascape that Crabbe knew, and to which Britten was drawn:

When Tides were neap, and, in the sultry day,
Through the tall-bounding Mud-banks made their way,
Which on each side rose swelling, and below
The dark warm Flood ran silently and slow;
There anchoring, Peter chose from Man to hide,
There hang his Head, and view the lazy Tide
In its hot slimy Channel slowly glide;
Where the small Eels that left the deeper way
For the warm Shore, within the Shallows play;
Where gaping Mussels, left upon the Mud,
Slope their slow passages to the fallen Flood; -
Here dull and hopeless he'll lie down and trace

[40.] 'Peter Grimes', Letter XXII, *The Borough*, 171–180. See Crabbe, *Poems*, 2015, p. 88.
[41.] Blunden, 1947, p. xviii.
[42.] Britten and Slater, 1961, p. 14.

How sidelong Crabs had scrawled their crooked race;
Or sadly listen to the tuneless cry
Of fishing Gull or clanging Golden-eye;
What time the Sea-birds to the Marsh would come,
And the loud Bittern, from the Bull-rush home;
Gave the Salt-ditch side the bellowing Boom:
He nursed the Feelings these dull Scenes produce,
And loved to stop beside the opening Sluice;[43]

Despite his later criticisms, it was for lines such as these that Francis Jeffrey, reviewing Crabbe's poems in *The Edinburgh Review* in 1808, described him as 'one of the most original [...] poets of the present century'.[44]

Crabbe and writing: What I thought I could best describe, that I attempted

In *The Borough*, as in *The Village* and *The Parish Register*, Crabbe drew upon the characters he had known and among whom he grew up. By contrast with the Romantics of his generation, he was an avowed realist – a chronicler of the world, and in particular of the human psyche. In November 1816, he received a letter from a Mrs Mary Leadbeater, writing from the Irish village of Ballitore (the same village, incidentally, in which Crabbe's patron Edmund Burke had been educated). She wanted to know whether his characters 'are drawn from life'.[45] Crabbe replied that he 'endeavoured to paint as nearly as I could and *dare*; for, in some Cases, I dared not'.

He added:

> There is not one of whom I had not in my Mind the Original, but I was obliged in most Cases to take them from their real Situations & in one or two Instances, even to change the Sex, and, in many the Circumstances. the nearest to real Life,

---

[43.] 'Peter Grimes', Letter XXII, *The Borough*, 181–200. See Crabbe, *Poems*, 2015, p. 88. Cf. Chapter 1, where the punctuation matches that of Forster's reprinted text.

[44.] Francis Jeffrey, unsigned review in *The Edinburgh Review*, Vol. 12, No. 23 (April 1808): p. 132.

[45.] Crabbe, *Life*, 1947 (1834), p. 198.

was the proud, ostentatious Man in the Borough [Sir Denys Brand, Letter XIII], who disguised a little Mind by doing great things; yet others were approaching to reality at greater or less Distances: indeed I do not know that I Could paint merely from my own Fancy & there is no Cause why we should. Is there not Diversity sufficient in society?[46]

What was *The Borough* about? Much of it is based on Aldeburgh, but is more than a depiction of that one town, drawing also on Beccles and Woodbridge. The twenty-four Letters making up the collection are a fictional expansion of Aldeburgh, incorporating Crabbe's experiences as a cleric and a villager in different parishes – as he notes in the preface, 'the reader is in some degree kept from view of any particular place'.[47] It is a place of officialdom but also of idiosyncrasy and downright oddness; as Alfred Ainger remarked: 'Besides church officials it exhibits every shade of the Nonconformist creed and practice, notably those of which the writer was now having unpleasant experience at Muston.'[48]

Like Crabbe's other imagined locations, the world of *The Borough* is a carefully drawn representation of provincial society. It has, Ainger continued:

> a mayor and corporation, and frequent parliamentary elections. It supports many professors of the law; physicians of high repute, and medical quacks of very low. Social life and pleasure is abundant, with clubs, card-parties, and theatres. It boasts an almshouse, hospital, prisons, and schools for all classes.[49]

In its colour and variety of social and professional life, Crabbe's *Borough* can be seen as a forerunner to the compendious and multilayered world of George Eliot's *Middlemarch* (1871).

[46.] Letter to Mary Leadbeater, 1 December 1816. See Crabbe, *Letters*, 1985, p. 203.
[47.] 'Preface', *The Borough*. See *Poetical Works*, 1932, p. 101.
[48.] Ainger, 1903, p. 109. Cf. Crabbe's critique of Nonconformist branches (Methodism he calls 'this spiritual influenza') in his Preface: *Poetical Works*, 1932, pp. 102–104.
[49.] Ibid, p. 109–10.

The Letters of the poem are imagined as written by an 'imaginary personage', a burgess of the town describing it for a friend.[50] Each deals with a separate topic. The characters include a dilettante vicar, an impoverished curate struggling to support a large family, and a parish clerk, as well as more marginal figures – an occupant of an almshouse, for example, and a condemned prisoner awaiting execution. As Crabbe himself stated in a notebook: 'I have chiefly, if not exclusively, taken my subjects and characters from that order of society where the least display of vanity is generally to be found, which is placed between the humble and the great.'[51]

His concern and compassion for the poor is a thread that runs through the poem's starkly depicted events. These sentiments crystallise in his condemnation of Suffolk's version of a workhouse, where there was no attempt to separate young and old, healthy and sick, or the criminal and the respectable.

> 'Tis cheerless living in such bounded view,
> With nothing dreadful, but with nothing new;
> Nothing to bring them joy, to make them weep;
> The day itself is, like the night asleep:[52]

Crabbe depicts what he sees and what he knows. As he explains in the preface:

> What I thought I could best describe, that I attempted; – the sea, and the country in the immediate vicinity; the dwellings, and the inhabitants; some incidents and characters, with an exhibition of morals and manners, offensive perhaps to those of extremely delicate feelings, but sometimes, I hope, neither unamiable nor unaffecting.[53]

The 'delicate feelings' of literary critics were, as we have seen, predictably offended – not least by the bleakness of Crabbe's outlook. Many of the characters of *The Borough* face retribution for their wrongdoings, forced

---

[50.] 'Preface', *The Borough*. See *Poetical Works*, 1932, p. 101.
[51.] Crabbe, *Life*, 1947 (1834), quoting from the poet's 'common-place book', p. 170.
[52.] 'The Poor and their Dwellings', Letter XVIII, *The Borough*. See *Poetical Works*, 1932, p. 180. Cf. Ainger, 1903, p. 121.
[53.] 'Preface', *The Borough*. See *Poetical Works*, 1932, p. 101.

to become outcasts from society and condemned to live with their thoughts in solitude, amid the unremitting rhythms of nature, bleak and unforgiving as these could be.

Crabbe's realism was partly to do with the place of his upbringing, in puritan and unpretentious East Anglia – 'not a sentimental province', in the words of Edmund Blunden.[54] It was also perhaps to do with his work as a doctor, the kind 'who calls on patients usually suspicious and reticent to hear them fully [...] and they will speak to him as one with higher powers than other men'.[55] Certainly he had an intimate knowledge of people. The character of Ellen Orford in Letter XX of *The Borough*, whose tale is one of four – including Peter Grimes – classified as 'The Poor of the Borough', is an old blind woman (by contrast with the schoolteacher of Britten's opera), recounting her life of woe – her illegitimate child, the realization that her child is an 'idiot', the seduction of that child by her brother. Her confidant, in this litany of misfortune, is her doctor.

Crabbe's harsh but sympathetic portrayal of the life of labourers, whether in the fields or on the shore, and their relationship with the natural world, can be traced back to his earliest work. In *The Village* (1783), he framed himself as a poet not of 'pleasing scenes' viewed from a distance but of real lives, viewed in close-up:

> *But when amid such pleasing scenes I trace*
> *The poor laborious natives of the place,*
> *And see the mid-day sun, with fervid ray,*
> *On their bare heads and dewy temples play; [...]*
> *Then shall I dare these real ills to hide,*
> *In tinsel trappings of poetic pride?*

Better those who escaped the ravages of this coast, as he himself eventually did, fleeing the shores 'where guilt and famine reign'.

> *Ah! hapless they who still remain;*
> *Who still remain to hear the ocean roar,*
> *Whose greedy waves devour the lessening shore;*
> *Till some fierce tide, with more imperious sway,*
> *Sweeps the low hut and all it holds away;*

[54.] Blunden, 1947, p. ix.
[55.] Ibid.

> *When the sad tenant weeps from door to door,*
> *And begs a poor protection from the poor.*[56]

That 'poor protection' was often, in reality, the village poorhouse. In Aldeburgh this was the sordid institution at the back of the town, close to where the library is now located, where in his early years Crabbe had frequently visited as a physician. In *The Village*, he evoked a place

> *whose walls of mud scarce bear the broken door;*
> *There, where the putrid vapours flagging, play,*
> *And the dull wheel hums doleful through the day;*
> *There children dwell who know no parents' care,*
> *Parents, who know no children's love, dwell there;*
> *Heart-broken matrons on their joyless bed,*
> *Forsaken wives and mothers never wed;*
> *Dejected widows with unheeded tears,*
> *And crippled age with more than childhood-fears;*
> *The lame, the blind, and, far the happiest they!*
> *The moping idiot and the madman gay.*[57]

Sympathetic to the plight of the poor, Crabbe was also cynical about those in authority. The parish doctor of *The Village* is 'all pride and business, bustle and conceit' – never mind that Crabbe had held the post himself – 'With looks unaltered by these scenes of woe, / With speed that entering, speaks his haste to go'. (Crabbe may here have been lampooning his former rival, Burham Raymond.) The fictional doctor descends from callousness into criminal negligence:

> *A potent quack, long versed in human ills,*
> *Who first insults the victim whom he kills;*
> *Whose murderous hand a drowsy bench protect,*
> *And whose most tender mercy is neglect.*[58]

The parish priest is little better. At a funeral of one of the sick:

> *The busy priest, detained by weightier care,*
> *Defers his duty till the day of prayer;*

[56.] *The Village*, Book I, 41–44, 47–48, 125–30. See Crabbe, *Poems*, 2015, p. 6, p. 9.
[57.] *The Village*, Book I, pp. 231–41. See Crabbe, *Poems*, 2015, p. 12.
[58.] *The Village*, Book I, 284–87: ibid, p. 13.

Character and Creation

And waiting long, the crowd retire distressed,
To think a poor man's bones should lie unblessed.[59]

Twenty-seven years on, *The Borough* unveils a similar cast of flawed characters, several of them eliciting empathy as much as censure. There is the parish clerk, Jachin, who plunders the church collection plate, forgetting to mute the sound of the gold coins dropping into his pocket by lining it with bran. He is caught in the act by an overseer of the parish, a righteous bully ('fond of Power, loud, lewd, and most severe') whose behaviour prompts the reader to side with the petty thief:

In wrath he rose, and thus his mind expressed.
'Foul Deeds are here!' and saying this he took
The Clerk, whose Conscience, in her cold-fit, shook;
His Pocket then was emptied on the place;
All saw his Guilt; all witnessed his Disgrace:
He fell, he fainted, not a groan, a look
Escaped the Culprit; 'twas a final stroke -
A death-wound never to be healed – a fall
That all had witnessed, and amazed were all.[60]

Jachin reaps his just deserts, discovering 'How much more fatal Justice is than Law'. Like Grimes, he is condemned to isolation in the purgatory of a bleak seascape, in which the changing climes of Aldeburgh's beach and estuary can readily be discerned:

In each lone place, dejected and dismayed,
Shrinking from view, his wasting Form he laid;
Or to the restless Sea and roaring Wind,
Gave the strong yearnings of a ruined Mind:
On the broad Beach, the silent Summer-day,
Stretched on some Wreck, he wore his Life away;
Or where the River mingles with the sea,
Or on the Mud-bank by the Elder-tree,
Or by the bounding Marsh-dyke, there was he:[61]

---

[59]. *The Village*, Book I, 345–48: ibid, p. 15.
[60]. 'The Parish-Clerk', Letter XIX, *The Borough*, 246–53. See Crabbe, *Poems*, 2015, p. 57.
[61]. 'The Parish-Clerk', Letter XIX, *The Borough*, 270–78: ibid, p. 58.

Others, too, err and suffer in a landscape that seems to reflect their inner dejection – such as Abel Keene, 'a poor Man, Teacher of a School of the lower Order'. Keene, growing nervous with the 'loud rebellious boys' in his charge, takes a job with a merchant 'where half the Labour brought him twice the Pay'.[62]

This respectable man escapes the stresses of the schoolroom for a quieter life as a bookkeeper. But craving companionship, Abel joins the merchant's son and his friends in their evening merrymaking, where he becomes a target for their mockery: they 'scorned as Fables all he held as true'. He abandons his values for the life of a debauched dandy. His pious sister urges him to repent:

> *What are thy Pleasures? – with the Gay to sit,*
> *And thy poor Brain torment for awkward Wit;*
> *All they good Thoughts (thou hat'st them) to restrain,*
> *And give a wicket Pleasure to the Vain;*
> *Thy long lean Frame by Fashion to attire,*
> *That Lads may laugh and Wantons may admire;*
> *To raise the mirth of Boys, and not to see,*
> *Unhappy Maniac! That they laugh at thee.*[63]

When the merchant dies, Keene's life unravels: he loses both his job and his new-found 'friends', and sinks into deep melancholy:

> *And now we saw him on the Beach reclined,*
> *Or causeless walking in the wintry Wind;*
> *And when it raised a loud and angry Sea,*
> *He stood and gazed, in wretched reverie:*
> *He heeded not the Frost, the Rain, the Snow,*
> *Close by the Sea he walked alone and slow:*
> *Sometimes his Frame through many an hour he spread*
> *Upon a Tomb-stone, moveless as the dead;*
> *And was there found a sad and silent place,*
> *There would he creep with slow and measured pace:*
> *Then would he wander by the River's side,*
> *And fix his eyes upon the falling Tide;*
> *The deep dry Ditch, the Rushes in the Fen,*
> *And mossy Crag-pits were his Lodgings then:*

---

[62] 'Abel Keene', Letter XXI, *The Borough*, 8: ibid, p. 71.
[63] 'Abel Keene', Letter XXI, *The Borough*, 16, 120–27: ibid, p. 72, p. 75.

> *There, to his discontented Thoughts a prey,*
> *The melancholy Mortal pined away.*[64]

Before long, Abel is discovered hanging in a pedlar's shed. It is a typical fate and moral reckoning for a Crabbe character – and one, as with Jachin and Grimes, inextricably linked with the locality. The 'Poor of the Borough' are, like the labourers pictured in *The Village*, 'cast by Fortune on a frowning coast / Which can no groves nor happy valleys boast'.

Crabbe's radical – unromantic – realism came to inspire the likes of Thomas Hardy. In a lecture at Aldeburgh Church in 2011, the writer Helen Lange drew parallels between the two men, their lives and their works. For both, she noted, *place* was of central importance: 'Hardy and Crabbe grew up in very different parts of rural England and of course at different times, but both had rural life deep in their souls and memories, and wrote about the people and places, the flora and fauna, without any sentiment and hardly any traces of idealism, but with closely observed realism.'[65]

Hardy visited Aldeburgh in 1905 for the 150th anniversary celebrations of Crabbe's birth taking place that year. He kept his programme from the event (now in the Dorset County Museum) and later commented on the occasion, saying he was 'honouring Crabbe as an apostle of realism who practised it in English Literature three-quarters of a century before the French realistic school had been heard of'.[66]

Leaving Suffolk: The seat of joy, the source of pain

Crabbe and his family left Rendham – and Suffolk – in 1805. His life after that was spent outside East Anglia, and yet his poems continued to evoke the place that had shaped him.

He had been obliged to return to his neglected parish of Muston in Leicestershire. This was quite different from Suffolk. Its surrounding landscape was 'open and uninteresting', Crabbe's son recalls. 'Here were

---

[64]. 'Abel Keene', Letter XXI, *The Borough*, 191–206: ibid, p. 77.
[65]. Helen Lange, 'Thomas Hardy and George Crabbe: The Native Environment Calls', *The Hardy Society Journal*, Vol. 7, No. 2 (Summer 2011): p. 38.
[66]. Ibid, p. 49.

no groves nor dry green lanes, nor gravel roads to tempt the pedestrian in all weather; but still the parsonage and its premises formed a pretty little oasis in the clayey desert.'[67]

Yet this was also the moment of Crabbe's literary revival, after a break of more than twenty years. His last publications had been *The Village* in 1783 and *The Newspaper* in 1785, after which he had immersed himself in the roles of parish priest and father. But all the while he had continued to write.

Then the first decade of the nineteenth century saw an outpouring of work, much of which had been started in Suffolk. It is thought that he began *The Parish Register* in 1802 and *The Borough* in 1804 – the poems were published in 1807 and 1810 respectively. *Sir Eustace Grey* was written in the winter of 1804–05.

Two years after his return to Muston, Crabbe's collected *Poems* were published by Hatchard on 29 October 1807. These featured *Sir Eustace Grey* and *The Parish Register*, together with revised versions of *The Village* and *The Library*. Francis Jeffrey – who would later review *The Borough* in somewhat caustic terms – was moved to praise him as 'one of the most original, nervous, and pathetic poets of the present century', contrasting the 'real life' of his poetry with the more interiorised and transcendental verse of 'Mr Wordsworth and his associates' – men who 'show us something that mere observation never yet suggested to anyone [...] more by eloquent and refined analysis of their own capricious feelings, than by any obvious or very intelligible ground of sympathy in their situation'.[68]

But noting Crabbe's apparent writer's block, Jeffrey lamented that it was 'upwards of twenty years since we were first struck with the vigour, originality, and truth of description of "The Village" and since we regretted that an author, who could write so well, should have written so little'. He added:

> From that time to the present, we have heard little of Mr Crabbe; and fear that he has been in a great measure lost sight of by the public, as well as by us. With a singular, and scarcely pardonable indifference to fame, he has remained, during this long interval, in patient or indolent repose; and, without making a single movement to maintain or advance the reputation he had acquired, has permitted others to usurp

---

[67] Crabbe, *Life*, 1947 (1834), p. 172.
[68] Jeffrey, 1808, p. 132, p. 133.

the attention which he was sure of commanding, and allowed himself to be nearly forgotten by a public, which reckons upon being reminded of all the claims which the living have on its favour.[69]

What had finally prompted Crabbe back into print? At least in part, the reason was practical: his younger son, John, then eighteen, was soon to go up to Cambridge and funds had to be found. The older son George had gone up in 1803.

Crabbe pleaded the excuse for his long silence – to his reading public – of a higher calling, namely his professional clerical duties. But he also suffered from lack of confidence: he no longer had a mentor. Burke had died in 1797 and Samuel Johnson in 1784 – and for a time he was without someone whose opinion he valued to read his work before publication.[70]

When living at Great Glemham years earlier (1796–1801) at the residence of Dudley North, Crabbe had renewed his acquaintance with the Whig statesman Charles James Fox (1749–1806), whom he had first met at Edmund Burke's house in 1781. Fox was a long-time proponent, who on one occasion at Great Glemham playfully pushed Crabbe ahead of himself while they were entering the dining room, declaring: 'If he had had his deserts, he would have walked before us all.'[71]

At Little Glemham in 1794, Fox had urged Crabbe to publish again, and had offered to look at any prospective writing and give his opinion. Crabbe did not take up the offer, feeling insufficiently prepared. As he finally assembled his new collection in 1806, Fox repeated his earlier offer – and so Crabbe sent him *The Parish Register* for comments. 'Whatever he approved,' Crabbe wrote in the preface to *Poems*, 'I have carefully retained; the parts he disliked are totally expunged.'[72] But Fox was terminally ill and died in the autumn of 1806. When Crabbe's

---

[69]. Ibid, p. 131.
[70]. By the time he penned his preface to *The Borough*, however, he would claim: 'I have lost some portion of the timidity once so painful, and [...] I am encouraged to take upon myself the decision of various points, which heretofore I entreated my friends to decide.' See Crabbe, *Poetical Works*, 1932, p. 100.
[71]. Mitford, 1834, p. 259.
[72]. Crabbe, 'Preface' in *Poems: by The Rev. George Crabbe LL. B.*, vol. 1 (London: Hatchard, 1810, fifth edition), p. xxviii.

collected volume was published the following year, he dedicated it to Fox's nephew and sometime ward, Henry Richard Vassall Fox, third Lord Holland.

By the time, then, that *The Borough* was published in 1810, Crabbe – as he admitted in the preface – had had 'less assistance from my friends', and yet he also insisted that readers should not conclude that it was written in haste, and that 'sufficient time and application were bestowed upon this work'.[73]

His sons were by now through Cambridge and – having followed their father into the church – had secured curacies in the Muston neighbourhood and come to live with him and Sarah. Life continued much as before: one benefit was that Crabbe was better able to pursue his botanical passions, thanks to a 'larger and better garden than in Suffolk'; here he 'passed much of his time amongst his choice weeds'.[74] But Sarah's health continued to decline. The family walks of old ceased to take place, although Crabbe still read aloud to the family in the evenings, winter or summer.

Crabbe's son recalls:

> Our front windows looked full on the churchyard, by no means like the common forbidding receptacles of the dead, but truly ornamental ground; for some fine elms partially concealed the small beautiful church and its spire, while the eye, travelling through their stems, rested on the banks of a stream and a picturesque old bridge.[75]

Meanwhile Crabbe's output continued. *The Borough* was followed by *Tales* in the summer of 1812, in the preface to which he defended his focus on the human, the psychological and the earthly, as opposed to the transcendental, spiritual or mystic. Francis Jeffrey, the critic who had lambasted *The Borough*, took a more circumspect view of *Tales* – calling Crabbe 'the most original writer who has ever come before us', but also complaining that the pieces 'are mere supplementary chapters to "the Borough", or "the Parish Register". The same tone – the same subjects – the same style, measure, and versification.'[76] And yet these

---

[73.] 'Preface', *The Borough*. See *Poetical Works*, 1932, pp. 100–101.
[74.] Crabbe, *Life*, 1947 (1834), p. 171.
[75.] Ibid, p. 172.
[76.] Francis Jeffrey, 'Tales: By the Reverend George Crabbe', *The Edinburgh Review*, Vol. 20, No. 40 (November 1812): p. 304, p. 278.

twenty-one verse stories did mark a departure – no longer focusing with the same intensity on the blighted lives of the poor, but drawing instead on the poet's own family life, or the lives of his acquaintances.

'The Parting Hour', for instance, is based on the picaresque experiences of his brother, William, who had become a sailor and been captured by the Spaniards, then taken to Mexico – where he became a silversmith and prospered, until his mounting riches drew accusations of Protestantism and he had to flee to Honduras. There, in 1803, an Aldeburgh sailor happened to meet him and told him that his eldest brother, George, was a clergyman. 'This cannot be *our* George,' declared William, 'he was a *Doctor!*'[77] No doubt Crabbe was equally incredulous at his brother's turns of fate.

Tales also included 'The Lover's Journey', in which a young man named John takes a morning ride to visit his beloved, Susan (those, at least, are their 'parish register' names: the lovers have graced each other with the names of Laura and Orlando). The tale clearly draws on Crabbe's early Aldeburgh days when he would travel twenty miles to Beccles to woo the young Sarah. With a characteristically acute observation of nature – in particular, the marshlands where he grew up – Crabbe captures the way in which the landscape is irradiated by the happy lover's eye:

> 'Various as beauteous, Nature, is thy face,'
> Exclaimed Orlando; 'all that grows has grace;
> All are appropriate – bog, and marsh, and fen,
> Are only poor to undiscerning men;
> Here may the nice and curious eye explore,
> How Nature's hand adorns the rushy moor;
> Here the rare moss in secret shade is found,
> Here the sweet myrtle of the shaking ground;'[78]

'The Parting Hour' tells the story of another Suffolk boy, Allen Booth, who leaves behind the sweetheart of his youth, Judith, for a career at sea. Returning forty years later, after captivity and exile – 'His mind oppress'd with woes and bent with age his frame' – Allen alights at the very place of his departure, Aldeburgh beach. Here he witnesses a lone unmanned vessel on the billowing waves, and in the other direction, another ghost – the town of his youth:

[77.] Crabbe, 1834, p. 175, n. 1.
[78.] 'The Lover's Journey', Tale X, *Tales*, 129–27. See Crabbe, *Poems*, 2015, pp. 234–35.

> O'er the black stern the moon-light softly played,
> The loosened foresail flapping in the shade:
> All silent else on shore: but from the town
> A drowsy peal of distant bells came down:
> From the tall houses here and there, a light
> Served some confused remembrance to excite:
> 'There', he observed, and new emotions felt,
> Was my first home – '[79]

The lines intimate Crabbe's own nostalgia for Aldeburgh, and a sense of the town being synonymous with his younger days. Those early experiences are even more pointedly evoked in 'The Patron', the story of a young poet taken up by a wealthy patron. This recalls, somewhat bitterly, Crabbe's introduction to high society during his chaplaincy at Belvoir Castle, his earlier attempts to gain a position, and – before that – his time as a labourer on Slaughden Quay, rolling butter tubs. Alfred Ainger has described the tale as 'powerful fiction rather than poetry', and yet the fictional element is (as often) no more than a veil over depths of emotional truth.[80]

John, the young man of 'The Patron', is cast in the mould of the young Crabbe: he 'felt not a love for money-making arts', and dedicated himself instead to the writing of poetry of a realist and satiric bent, entertaining a propensity for fanciful visions of future success.

The tale recounts how John, the son of a 'Borough-burgess', helps a local lord by writing supportive verses at election time – and in return is invited to pay a visit of some weeks to the lord's country seat where he falls in love, unrequited, with the nobleman's daughter. Her father, Lord Frederick, meanwhile undertakes to find the aspiring poet a suitable post. After a while, however, the family leaves for London – the squire insisting that he will not forget his new *protégé*. Three months elapse ('every day / Drew from the sickening hopes their strength away'). Finally, John receives a letter inviting him to town. He waits at the lord's mansion in a cold, fireless room and after several hours is told to come back on another day. Again, Lord Frederick fails to see him and instead passes him a letter, advising him to abandon his dreams. Soon after, John finds himself fallen into 'some appointment on the London Quays', disgraced and disillusioned.[81]

---

[79] 'The Parting Hour', *Tale* II, 203–10. See Crabbe, *Poems*, 2015, p. 118–19.
[80] Ainger, 1903, p. 137.
[81] 'The Patron', Tale V, *Tales*, 568. See Crabbe, *Poems*, 2015, p. 172.

Character and Creation

John returns to his parents' home where he becomes 'afflicted and subsumed / By hunger, sorrow, cold, and solitude'. Sunk into depression, he dies. His father gives thanks to God, as he leaves his son's grave, that he has no other sons with talents and desires above their station. One senses Crabbe's painful intuition that this could have been his own fate. And the laments of the bereaved father might well reflect the poet's view of his own father's antipathy:

> 'There lies my Boy,' he cried, 'of care bereft,
> And, Heaven be praised, I've not a genius left:
> No one among ye, Sons! Is doomed to live
> On high-raised hopes of what the Great may give;'[82]

As for the Patron, Crabbe imagines an outpouring of belated regret – tinged with vanity – upon his hearing of the young man's death:

> My Lord, to whom the Poet's fate was told,
> Was much affected, for a man so cold;
> 'Dead!' said his Lordship, 'run distracted, mad!
> Upon my soul I'm sorry for the lad;
> And now, no doubt, th'obliging world will say,
> That my harsh usage help'd him on his way;
> What! I suppose, I should have nursed his muse,
> And with champagne have brighten'd up his views;
> Then had he made me famed my whole life long,
> And stunned my ears with gratitude and song.
> Still should the father hear that I regret
> Our joint misfortune – Yes! I'll not forget –'[83]

In the *Tales*, there is often the same pattern of error and retribution – or at least of fated consequences – as seen in *The Borough*. In 'Edward Shore', the protagonist seduces his close friend's wife: his decline through drink follows, and a descent into madness. In 'The Learned Boy', a farmer's son, Stephen, falls in with the wrong set and becomes an atheist – a stance that incurs a cruel and excessive beating from his father with echoes of the transgressions of Peter Grimes.

Many of the poems deal with sadness and infirmity, whether spiritual or physical. The Romantic poet Robert Southey summed these aspects

---

[82.] 'The Patron', Tale V, *Tales*, 718–21: ibid, p. 176.
[83.] 'The Patron', Tale V, *Tales*, 704–15: ibid.

up in 1808 (by way of a contrast with Oliver Goldsmith), imputing to Crabbe a darkness as much psychological as literal, present even in his moments of lightness:

> Goldsmith threw a sunshine over all his pictures, like that of one of our water-colour artists when he paints for ladies – a light and beauty not to be found in Nature, though not more brilliant or beautiful than what Nature really affords; Crabbe's have a gloom which is also not in Nature – not the shade of a heavy day, of mist, or of clouds, but the dark and overcharged shadows of one who paints by lamplight – whose very lights have a gloominess. In part this is explained by his history.[84]

* * *

One part of that history, of course, was Sarah – and her long descent into depression. In the summer of 1813, as her health deteriorated, she expressed a wish to see London once more. And so the family spent nearly three months in a hotel just off the Strand, during which time Crabbe was able to visit Dudley North and other old friends. He did not omit to visit the London poor – 'not unmindful of his own want and misery in the great city thirty years before'.[85]

The family returned to Muston in late August, and just weeks later Sarah died aged sixty-three, on 21 September 1813.[86] She was buried at Muston Church. Despite the long years of her mental illness and the care demanded of Crabbe during this time, her death came as a blow. Two days later, he himself developed 'an alarming illness' resembling acute cholera. 'He appeared regardless of life,' his son recalls, 'and desired, with the utmost coolness, that my mother's grave might not be closed till it was seen whether he should recover.'[87]

Neil Powell speculates that he had brought back some kind of virus from London which proved fatal to his wife but which he, in better health, was able to survive.[88] Either way, Sarah's death marked the end of a long chapter in his life, one that had begun in Parham in 1772 with

---

[84.] Robert Southey, letter to Neville White, 30 September 1808, quoted in Ainger, 1903, p. 146.
[85.] Ainger, 1908, p. 147.
[86.] Powell, 2014, p. 243 – correcting the son's date of 21 October 1813.
[87.] Crabbe, *Life*, 1947 (1834), p. 182.
[88.] Powell, 2014, p. 243.

Character and Creation 133

a rapidly blossoming love, and that had latterly transformed into a slow and painful decline. Robert Southey noted in his letter of 1808: 'his wife became deranged, and when all this was told me by one who knew him well, five years ago, he was still almost confined in his own house, anxiously waiting upon this wife in her long and hopeless malady. A sad history! It is no wonder that he gives so melancholy a picture of human life.'[89]

Crabbe recovered, at least physically, although the process was gradual. 'His demeanour, while the danger lasted, was that of perfect humility, but of calm hope, and unshaken firmness.'[90] But Sarah's death marked the onset of a profound melancholy. The loneliness of life in Muston began to weigh on him, as his son notes, and he acknowledged that the parish was 'no longer what it has been to me: I am now a solitary with a social disposition, – a hermit without a hermit's resignation'.[91]

In a cruel confirmation of the theme of 'The Lover's Journey' and many other poems – that outward sights are transformed (made lovely or melancholic) by inner mood – the places and activities that had once been stimuli for Crabbe lost their allure. 'His garden had become indifferent to him,' recounts his son,

> nor was that occupation ever resumed again: besides, that diversity of religious sentiment, which I mentioned before, had produced a coolness in some of his parishioners, which he felt the more painfully, because whatever might be their difference of opinion, he was ever ready to help and oblige them all by medical and other aid to the utmost extent of his power. They carried this unkind feeling so far as to ring the bells for his successor, before he himself had left the residence.[92]

---

[89] Robert Southey, letter to Neville White, 30 September 1808, quoted in Powell, 2004, pp. 243–44.
[90] Crabbe, *Life*, 1947 (1834), p. 183.
[91] Ibid, p. 186.
[92] Ibid, p. 183. The younger Crabbe alludes here to his father's discovery, on returning to Muston, that numerous parishioners had defected to the Methodist church.

Alienated from his pastimes and parishioners, Crabbe became morbid – predicting that he would not live longer than six or seven years, and often saying: 'life is as tedious as a twice-told tale'.[93]

But as at other dark moments in his life, there came a fortuitous turn. Not long after he had recovered sufficiently to resume his clerical duties, a letter arrived from an old friend. This was the fifth Duke of Rutland, John Henry Manners, in whose father's house and care Crabbe had lived at the start of his marriage. The young Duke offered him the living of the county town of Trowbridge, Wiltshire, in exchange for the one in Muston. That was needed for the Reverend Henry Byron, a cousin of Lord Byron. Crabbe was amenable to the swap; he had fallen out of love with Muston and actively welcomed the prospect of Trowbridge: 'My father looked to a new residence without that feeling of regret which generally accompanies even an advantageous removal in later life".[94]

Once more, Crabbe's circumstances were radically to change. He was now set to leave Leicestershire. But as he prepared to go, he wanted to pay one more visit to Aldeburgh to see his sister, 'from whom he was to be still more widely divided'. He spent a day in a solitary ramble among the scenery of 'bygone years': Parham and the woods of Glemham, at that time in the first blossom of May. He did not return until night. In his notebook he wrote the following nostalgic lines, evoking his life with Sarah and her loss – as well as his sense of a final departure:

> Yes, I behold again the place,
> The seat of joy, the source of pain;
> It brings in view the form and face
> That I must never see again.
>
> The night-bird's song that sweetly floats
> On this soft look – this balmy air,
> Brings to the mind her sweeter notes
> That I again must never hear.
>
> Lo! yonder shines that window's light,
> My guide, my token, heretofore;
> And now again it shines as bright,
> When those dear eyes can shine no more.

[93.] Ibid, p. 187.
[94.] Ibid, p. 183.

> *Then hurry from this place away!*
> *It gives not now the bliss it gave:*
> *For Death has made its charm his prey,*
> *And joy is buried in her grave.*[95]

Crabbe was inducted to the Trowbridge church by the curate, the Reverend Fletcher on 3 June 1814. In his new surroundings, he remained subject to fits of melancholy; but gradually these lessened and 'he became contented and cheerful, and I hope I may add,' writes his son, 'positively happy'. He was gratified by the affections of the 'most cultivated families' of the town, and by 'the attentions of the young and gay among them [...] finding the old satirist in many things very different from what they had looked for'. Indeed, the old satirist's spirits were rejuvenated: 'he had recovered not only the enjoyment of sound health, but much of the vigour and spirit of youthful feelings'.[96]

Not that the move to Trowbridge was entirely smooth. As in former parishes, Crabbe found it hard to win over the general populace, despite his popularity among the principal households. His immediate predecessor, the curate of the previous rector, had been liked and universally respected – and favoured as the next pastor. The Duke of Rutland's awarding of the position to Crabbe had not gone down well. Gossip and rumours were put about that Crabbe was a dissipated man, a dandy and a gambler. He declined to play politics, however; and would offend through 'impolitic frankness'.[97]

[95.] Quoted in ibid, p. 185. There are shades here of Thomas Hardy's poem 'At Castle Boterel' (1913), in which the author, coming to a stretch of road, remembers a fleeting romantic encounter on the same route long ago. In the final stanza, he watches the memory recede:

> *I look and see it there, shrinking, shrinking,*
> *I look back at it amid the rain*
> *For the very last time; for my sand is sinking,*
> *And I shall traverse old love's domain*
> *Never again.*

[96.] Ibid, p. 185, p. 187.

[97.] Ibid, p. 188.

On top of all this, he embraced the cause of a political candidate who had aroused the hostility of the prevailing manufacturing interest in the locality. And finally, 'in a town remarkable for diversity of sects and warmth of discussion, [he] adhered [...] to the same view of scriptural doctrines which had latterly found little favour even at Muston'.

Crabbe's religious approach was to urge 'his flock to virtuous conduct, by placing a future award ever full in their view, instead of dwelling on the temporal motives rendered so prominent at that time by many of his brethren'.[98] In short, he cut a figure much like that of his own Rector in *Tales of the Hall* (1819) – advocating self-denial and a simple moral code:

> 'A moral teacher!' Some, contemptuous, cried;
> He smiled, but nothing of the fact denied,
> Nor, save by his fair life, to charge so strong replied.
> Still, though he bade them not on aught rely
> That was their own, but all their worth deny,
> They call'd his pure advice his cold morality;
> [...]
> 'Heathens,' they said, 'can tell us right from wrong,
> But to a Christian higher points belong.'[99]

In time, though, Crabbe's liberal and tolerant approach to critics and dissenters won people round. Those same character traits that had at first aroused hostility gradually endeared him to his congregation. They included his 'boldness and uncompromising perseverance in the midst of opposition and reproach', together with his consistent and fearless support, despite hostility and riots, for John Benett (the Whig candidate to whom manufacturers were opposed), and finally, his steadfast religious opinions, which gained respect if not broad sympathy. 'They who differed from him admitted that he had a right also to his own religious and political opinions. His integrity and benevolence were justly appreciated; his talents acknowledged, and his disposition loved.'[100]

* * *

---

[98] Crabbe, *Life*, 1947 (1838), p. 139.

[99] 'The Natural Death of Love', Book XIV, *Tales of the Hall*. See Crabbe, *Poetical Works*, 1932, pp. 437–38.

[100] Crabbe, *Life*, 1947 (1834), p. 191.

Crabbe's regained peace and spiritual steadfastness seem to have been reflected outwardly. 'Perhaps,' continues his son, 'he had never looked so well, in many respects, as he did about this time; his temples getting more bare, the height of his well-developed forehead appeared as increased, and more than ever like one of those heads by which Wilkie [Sir David Wilkie, the portrait painter, 1785–1841] makes so many converts to the beauty of human decay.' Physically, Crabbe had become stouter, 'though without fatness'; and 'although he began to stoop, his limbs and motions were strong and active'.[101]

[101.] Ibid, p. 188.

Figure 17. George Crabbe by Henry William Pickersgill, c. 1818–19

Chapter 6

Endings and Beginnings

Bath and London: I am something of a novelty

Crabbe's move to Wiltshire in 1814, at the age of almost sixty, marked the start of a new life – and a new lease of life. Geographically, socially and spiritually, the setting was far removed from his native east coast. But this late chapter was an eventful and important one which throws his earlier Suffolk years into sharp relief. He was quickly admitted into the affections of the cultivated families of Trowbridge. He would also make regular trips to London where he met the famous personages of the day and mingled in high society. It was not his natural milieu, but his reputation and learning enabled him to fit in, and he relished the experience.

'In appearance, manners, and disposition, he was entirely the gentleman,' relates his son, remarking on the ease with which Crabbe took to fashionable company, and pointing out moreover that the seeds of his social aptitude had been sown early:

> Mr Burke had discovered this stamp when [Crabbe] had recently left the warehouse at Slaughden, and since that time [...] his profession, his studies, his age, and his literary success had fully ripened the character. Perhaps it may be said, that no one so humbly born and bred, ever retained so few traces of his origin.[1]

Crabbe's learning and bearing allowed him to 'pass' in almost any circle:

---

[1] Crabbe, *Life*, 1947 (1834), p. 205.

> His person and his countenance peculiarly led the mind from the suspicion of any, but a highly cultivated and polished education; venerable, clerical, intellectual – it seemed a strange inconsistency to imagine him, even in early youth, occupied as a warehouseman; and, in fact, there was no company in which his appearance would not have proclaimed him an equal.[2]

Trowbridge was situated close to Bath, Bowood and other small centres of cultivation. Crabbe enjoyed frequent trips to the theatre in Bath and by degrees was absorbed into the yet more 'distinguished society of London', visiting for several successive seasons. It was a life of meetings in coffee houses, breakfasts with the titled, and dining at their homes – perhaps as removed as can be imagined from the hard labour of rolling butter tubs on Slaughden Quay.

All the same, one suspects that Crabbe held on to the advice that the father in 'The Patron' confers on his son, not to be in thrall to the aristocracy:

> 'Strive not too much for favour; seem at ease,
> And rather pleased thyself, than bent to please:
> Upon thy Lord with decent care attend,
> But not too near; thou canst not be a friend.'[3]

And again, on the importance of circumspection:

> 'Observe the Prudent; they in silence sit,
> Display no learning and affect no wit;
> They hazard nothing, nothing they assume,
> But know the useful art of acting dumb.
> Yet to their eyes each varying look appears,
> And every word finds entrance at their ears.'[4]

Crabbe had a sense of his own underlying difference from the notables with whom he was mingling. A hint of that self-awareness can be found in a remark he penned in a letter of July 1817: 'This visit to London has, indeed, been a rich one. I had new things to see, and was, perhaps, something of a novelty myself.'[5]

[2.] Ibid.
[3.] 'The Patron', Tale V, *Tales*, 273–76. See Crabbe, *Poems*, 2015, p. 163.
[4.] 'The Patron', Tale V, *Tales*, 315–20: ibid, p. 164.
[5.] Letter of 25 July 1817. Quoted in Crabbe, *Life*, 1947 (1834), p. 222

And yet his son notes that things were now very different from those earlier years when Crabbe would sit 'at the tables of Mr Burke, Sir Joshua Reynolds and the Duke of Rutland' as an unproved talent. Back then, he was under the patronage of people who gained him admission to their prestigious set. But when he returned to high society in later life, it was his own poetic reputation that procured him access.[6]

Recalling the observation of a friend, Crabbe's son gives an insight into the figure his father cut in society at this time:

> There can be no doubt that he produced a very pleasing impression on those who now, for the first time, beheld and heard him. There was much of the old school in his manners, and even in the disposition of his beautiful white hair; but this sat gracefully on his time of life and professional character, and an apparent simplicity, arising from his strangeness to some of the recent modes of high life, was mingled with so much shrewdness of remark, that most people found his conversation irresistibly amusing.[7]

Crabbe's 'London Journal' from 1817 details some of those he met and dined with. They included the Lansdowne family (whose family seat was the magnificent Bowood House in Wiltshire, now largely demolished, and whose palatial London residence nowadays houses the exclusive Lansdowne Club) through to the Reverend William Lisle Bowles – an antiquarian and poet whose edited volume of Alexander Pope ignited a prolonged literary controversy – and Samuel Rogers, another poet who introduced Crabbe to 'scores of famous people in the social, political, and literary circles of the city'.[8]

Another name in Crabbe's journal was that of Countess Bessborough – Henrietta ('Harriet') Ponsonby – notorious for her prolific love affairs – who is reputed to have professed: 'I can never love anyone just *a little*'. (Bessborough was the mother of Lady Caroline Lamb, herself famous for a love affair with Lord Byron, of whom she claimed to have coined the phrase, 'mad, bad and dangerous to know'.) Lord and Lady Holland, who hosted regular political and intellectual soirees at Holland House,

---

[6.] Ibid, p. 203.
[7.] Crabbe, *Life*, 1947 (1834), p. 206.
[8.] Crabbe, *Letters*, 1985: Appendix, p. 407.

were also close acquaintances. It was to Lord Holland – Henry Richard Vassall Fox – that Crabbe had dedicated *The Parish Register* in 1807, in light of the long-term support of his uncle, Charles James Fox.

In the spring of 1822, Crabbe met Sir Walter Scott (1771–1832), and later that year visited him at home in Edinburgh, where he encountered the celebrated novelist among a circle of clansmen friends. Crabbe recorded in his journal from the trip: 'Sir Walter was the life and soul of the whole'. A letter to Crabbe's son from John Gibson Lockhart (who edited and revised the former's biography of the poet) describes the visit to Scotland and Crabbe's demeanour at that time:

> The image of your father, then first seen, but long before admired and revered in his works, remains as fresh as if the years that have now passed were but so many days. – His noble forehead, his bright beaming eyes without any thing of old age about it - though he was then, I presume, above seventy - his tones of his voice – all are reproduced the moment I open any page of his poetry: and how much better have I understood and enjoyed his poetry, since I was able thus to connect with it the living presence of the man![9]

Lockhart further reminisced that when Crabbe came down for breakfast, Sir Walter had not yet appeared and the poet found before him three 'portly personages all in full Highland garb' and 'talking in a language he did not understand; so he never doubted they were foreigners'. The letter adds: 'The Celts, on their part, conceived Mr Crabbe, dressed as he was in rather an old-fashioned style of clerical prosperity, with buckles in his shoes, for instance, to be some learned *abbé*, who had come on a pilgrimage to the shrine of Waverley.'

When Sir Walter and his family entered the room a little later, he found Crabbe and 'these worthy lairds hammering away, with pain and labour, to make themselves mutually understood in most execrable French. Great was the relief, and potent the laughter, when the host interrupted their colloquy with his plain English "Good-morning".'[10]

In his early years at Trowbridge, Crabbe was introduced to Hannah Hoare, second wife of the Quaker banker Samuel Hoare – a prominent abolitionist. Their home in Hampstead was, like that of the Hollands,

---

[9] John Gibson Lockhart, letter to George Crabbe Jr., 26 December 1833. See Crabbe, *Life*, 1947 (1834), p. 242.

[10] Ibid, p. 243.

Endings and Beginnings

a fertile meeting ground for the political and cultural elites. Crabbe became a regular visitor to Heath House from 1817, where social occasions were akin to a real-life *Vanity Fair*. The Hoares also had a family home, Cliff House, at Cromer in Norfolk, where Crabbe was a guest on several occasions.[11] Hannah and her daughter later published Samuel's memoirs, where they refer to 'a drawing, dated November 1822, [which] represents Crabbe walking with Sarah Hoare in the field by Cliff House. With them are Mrs [Amelia] Opie, Samuel Hoare, [William] Wilberforce and Dr. [Stephen] Lushington.'[12] This gathering of progressives was probably typical of such stays.

The names of those Crabbe met were a roll-call of the famous and influential of the day. They included leading politicians such as the Tory statesman George Canning, Henry Brougham (later, as Lord Chancellor, to play a leading role in the Reform Act of 1832 and the Slavery Abolition Act of 1833) and the Duke of Wellington, who had led the victory against Napoleon in 1815.[13] Also gracing the Hoares' London salon were philanthropists such as the abolitionist William Wilberforce – one of the walkers at Cromer – and writers such as Byron, Scott, Wordsworth and Thomas Campbell. Crabbe continued to visit each year until 1830, notwithstanding a fallout with the Hoares ('a peevish and now regretted misunderstanding', as he later recalled) over a missed dinner date.[14]

---

[11] Powell, 2004, p. 273.

[12] Sarah Hoare, Hannah Hoare, 'Preface' in *Memoirs of Samuel Hoare by his Daughter Sarah and his Widow Hannah* (London: Headley Brothers, 1911), p. xi. Lushington, a prominent judge, and Opie, a novelist, both appear in Benjamin Robert Haydon's painting *The Anti-Slavery Society Convention* (1840).

[13] Crabbe, *Letters*, 1985: Appendix, pp. 397–98.

[14] Letter to Elizabeth Charter, 7 August 1817. See Crabbe, *Letters*, 1985, pp. 227–28. Campbell later recalled, in a letter to the poet's son: 'The first time I met Crabbe was at Holland House, where he and Tom Moore [the Irish writer] and myself lounged the better part of a morning about the park and library [...] His mildness in literary argument struck me with surprise in so stern a poet of nature.' Quoted in Crabbe, *Life*, 1947 (1834), p. 211.

The poet relished the opportunities of his new life – observing, in a modification of Johnson's famous dictum, 'yet I love London; and who does not, if not confined to it?'[15] Not that the social whirlwind was a distraction from his vocation; he was still writing, and strove to complete thirty lines a day.

Was Crabbe a changed man, with all this mixing in the circles of the monied and titled? Not according to his son:

> When he returned home after one of these intoxicating visits to the metropolis, no one could trace the slightest difference in his manners or habits. He rarely spoke, even to his sons, of the brilliant circles in which he had been figuring; [...] He resumed next morning, just as if nothing had happened, his visits among his parishioners, his care of parish business, his books and papers, and last, not least, his long rambles among the quarries near Trowbridge.[16]

Those visits to the quarries did indicate one altered habit, however. After the death of Sarah, he did not return to botany, but instead took up fossils: 'Fossils were thence to him what weeds and flowers had been: he would spend hours on hours hammer in hand, not much pleased if anyone interrupted him, rarely inviting either my brother or myself to accompany him.'[17]

He also continued to dedicate himself to his role as vicar, applying himself with zeal to his ministerial duties: he was attentive to the many parishioners who called at the house, forbidding the servants from dismissing them, and helping out with money as well as counsel.

Meanwhile, in the spring of 1815, Crabbe's clergyman sons – who had accompanied him to Trowbridge – had both decided to travel. Aware that they would soon be settling for life in a village parsonage, they felt 'that this was the only opportunity of seeing something of our native country', and they both left Wiltshire for two years. It is possible that their father's new social connections and diversions were a factor in their decision to leave: they could be safe in the knowledge that he was absorbed both by his duties and lighter amusements.[18] John, the

---

[15.] Crabbe, *Life*, 1947 (1834), p. 218.

[16.] Ibid, p. 225.

[17.] Ibid, p. 226.

[18.] Ibid, p. 191.

younger brother, married in 1816 and returned to serve as his father's curate. The following year, George Crabbe junior married and settled within twenty miles, in the curacy of Pucklechurch.

Crabbe and women:
Oh! For some Made-on-purpose-Creature

Mr. Crabbe was not at all averse to the circulation of the bottle, and his Suffolk neighbours often mention some of his feats, while the old ladies in the eastern part of the county still remark the attractive warmth of his manners to them, when he joined them from the dinner table. 'D——n it, Sir,' said a Suffolk 'squire to us the other day, 'the only day Crabbe ever dined with me, he made love to my sister.' There are some ladies even now near us, who inform us with smiles (being assured of their safety) that they have been frightened at his warmth.[19]

Crabbe had travelled a long way. The West Country, with its gentle contours and yellowish limestone, contrasted with the dullness of Muston – and was even further removed from the harsh flint and bleakness of the East Anglian coast. But the picturesque charm of his new surroundings, coupled with the gregariousness and gaiety of his new life, only served to underline Crabbe's loneliness.

He had been devoted to Sarah and attentive to her throughout the years of her mental decline – what is now thought to have been a severe and prolonged case of bipolar disorder. A few weeks after her death in the autumn of 1813, he admitted – in a letter to an old friend – "She has been dying these ten years":

> I cannot weigh sorrows in a Ballance or make Comparisons between different Kinds of Affliction, nor do I judge whether I should have suffered most to have parted with my poor Sally, as I did part (if indeed such was parting) or to have seen her pass away with all her Faculties, feelings, senses acute & awake as my own.

[19.] Mitford, 1834, p. 257, footnote.

The friend in whom Crabbe was confiding was Alethea Lewis, previously Alethea Brereton, the woman who had introduced him to Sarah at Parham forty years earlier ('nor does Life appear short,' he wrote at the start of his letter: 'it seems a long time since I met [you] for the first Interview').[20] Back then, she had been engaged to his fellow apprentice surgeon, William Springall Levett, who died young in 1774. Fourteen years later, she married Augustus Lewis, a surgeon at Peasenhall, Suffolk, and emigrated to America, but returned for reasons of health after just a year; she then went on to become a prolific novelist, both anonymously and under the pseudonym Eugenia de Acton – publishing ten novels and a volume of essays.

As one of the Crabbes' earliest friends, Lewis – known as Stella in their Parham days – was well placed to comprehend the scale of his loss. The move to Trowbridge in 1814 accentuated that loss but it was a time of flourishing epistolary friendships with women. As Crabbe wrote to Mary Leadbeater two years after the move:

> *Our*, I could once say, but I am alone now, & thus removing into a busy Town among the Multitude the Loneliness is more apparent & more melancholy, but this is only at certain Times & then I have, though at considerable Distances six female Friends, unknown to each other but all dear very dear to me.[21]

Leadbeater, whose family were Quakers from Ballitore, had first met Crabbe at Edmund Burke's London house in St James' Square in 1784. She had then been on a tour of England with her father, Richard Shackleton, Burke's former schoolmaster. In 1791, she married William Leadbeater, a former pupil of her father and a Ballitore yeoman farmer – and became a writer. Her correspondence with Crabbe began when she wrote to him in November 1816 – asking whether he based his characters on real-life individuals; the quotation above derives from Crabbe's enthusiastic reply (which opens: 'Mary Leadbeater! – Yes indeed I do well remember

---

[20.] Letter to Alethea Brereton Lewis, 25 October 1813. See Crabbe, *Letters*, 1985, p. 117. Cf. Whitehead, 1995, p. 214.

[21.] Letter to Mary Leadbeater, 1 December 1816. See Crabbe, *Letters*, 1985, p. 204.

Endings and Beginnings

You!').[22] Their exchange of letters persisted over ten years, prompting multiple insights from Crabbe regarding his own poetry and literature in general.

As Crabbe intimated to Leadbeater, he had embarked on flirtations with several women. He had always preferred the company of women, a fact that his son relates in what now seem strikingly outmoded terms: 'all his most intimate friends ... were ladies', and 'he loved the very failings of the female mind: men in general appeared to him too stern, reserved, unyielding and worldly; and he ever found relief in the gentleness, the tenderness and the unselfishness of woman'.[23]

Or, as Crabbe himself had put it to one of these confidantes, Elizabeth Charter, in a letter the previous summer:

> Oh! For some Made-on-purpose-Creature whom I might at my own will though with all respectful freedom, sit with & walk & read or hear [or] be silent just as the Humour & Spirit prompted & for whom I should feel the partiality and affection that gives such Interest to these Conversations & to this Silence.[24]

It was a time of romantic anguish. Crabbe seems to have fallen more than once into the classic syndrome of the older man infatuated with a far younger woman, becoming as besotted and at times irrational as a young lover. His son wrote: 'I cannot but consider it as a very interesting trait in the history of his mind, that he was capable at so late a stage [he was 62], of feeling [...] so exactly as a man of five-and-twenty would have done under the same circumstances.'[25]

There were at least half a dozen women with whom Crabbe had dalliances. Charlotte Campion Williams was the daughter of a wealthy owner of mines in Cornwall. They started corresponding in 1813, the

---

[22.] Ibid, p. 201.
[23.] Crabbe, *Life*, 1947 (1834), p. 192. Cf. Crabbe's own assessment of his partiality, in his first letter to Leadbeater: 'With Men I do not much associate, not as deserting & much less as disliking the male part of Society, but as being unfit for it; not hardy, nor grave, not knowing enough nor sufficiently acquainted with the Everyday Business and concerns of Men; but my beloved Creatures have Minds with which I can better assimilate.' Crabbe, *Letters*, 1985, p. 204.
[24.] Letter to Elizabeth Charter, 6 June 1815. See Crabbe, *Letters*, 1985, p. 177.
[25.] Crabbe, *Life*, 1947 (1834), p. 195.

year Crabbe's wife died, after Charlotte – an admirer of his poetry – sent him a story of romance among miners. Crabbe was a popular poet of the day and she thought the story suited to his style of composition.

Their exchange of letters lasted several months. But Charlotte was engaged and her fiancé (moved by disapproval and no doubt some jealousy) advised her to drop the correspondence, thinking the missives 'nothing less than love letters'.[26] His intuition was correct: Crabbe then wrote a letter proposing to visit that was also a clear declaration of love.[27]

Charlotte at this time had a friend staying with her, also Charlotte, the daughter of John and Caroline Ridout of Baughurst, Hampshire. The first Charlotte begged her friend to write to Crabbe and, in essence, break off the correspondence by informing him that she was engaged. This the second Charlotte (Ridout) did with great tact and flattery. So well did she perform the task and so delighted was Crabbe with her letter that he simply transferred his affections: according to the memoirist Mrs John Farrar (a close friend of Sarah Hoare) in her anecdotal *Recollections* of 1865, he switched 'his proposals from the first Charlotte to the second; he was sure they were kindred spirits, and as he had not seen either lady, it would make no difference to him!'[28]

Charlotte Ridout was clearly more amenable, however, than her friend. She and Crabbe met and they became engaged in September 1814. The wedding was fixed for a date a few months ahead, and Charlotte went ahead with preparations. The wedding cake had already been baked, white gloves bought for the guests, and guest favours – bows of white satin ribbon, edged with a silver fringe – were being made when news suddenly reached Charlotte that the engagement was off.

Whether Crabbe had thought better of marriage with a young girl in her twenties, or been persuaded against it, or both, is not clear. Unfortunately, Charlotte had not taken his earlier hints. As Mrs Farrar recounted:

> It appeared afterwards that Crabbe's grown up sons convinced him of the folly of his conduct; he had long repented of his sudden engagement, and had tried by his correspondence so to displease the lady, as to make her break it off. She was resolved to have the *éclat* of marrying a celebrated poet, and

---

[26.] Powell, 2004, p. 238.

[27.] This is detailed by Mrs John Farrar, a friend of Sarah Hoare's, in *Recollections of Seventy Years* (Boston: Ticknor and Fields, 1866), pp. 67–68.

[28.] Ibid, p. 68.

would take no hints to the contrary. She was also in love with her old bard, and never recovered from her chagrin and sorrow. She died in a few years and her family always believed that her life was shortened by this affair.

Mrs. Farrar met with Crabbe some time after the unfortunate episode: 'In a few days we had talked over the whole affair of Miss Charlotte, and he ended by saying, "I know I behaved very badly, but I should have done worse if I had married her".'[29]

The flirtations with the two Charlottes must have been an embarrassment to Crabbe's family and are barely mentioned in his son's biography. Their true feelings are hard to gauge in the latter's anodyne statement:

> I have [...] no great wish to dwell on the subject; though, I must add, it was one that never for a moment disturbed the tranquillity of his family; nay, that, on one occasion at least, my brother and myself looked with sincere pleasure to the prospect of seeing our father's happiness increased by a new alliance.[30]

Another, more enduring relationship was with Charter, who met Crabbe in the winter of 1814–15. She was in her early thirties, a little older than Charlotte Ridout, and at the time she was acting as companion and adviser to her brother-in-law, General William Peachey. It was at his residence in Bath that Crabbe met Elizabeth. For more than a decade, they were close friends and correspondents. According to Neil Powell, she was 'arguably the second great love of Crabbe's life', and although they did not marry, she 'would be closer to his inner self even than his sons'.[31]

The letters he wrote to Elizabeth Charter provide a revealing glimpse into Crabbe's evolving feelings. In one, he recollects his recent infatuation with Charlotte Williams – the first of the two Charlottes – confessing that as their correspondence proceeded, he had indulged an unrealistic fantasy that she would overlook their age gap:

[29.] Ibid, pp. 68–71. Quoted in Crabbe, *Letters*, 1985, p. 406–407.
[30.] Crabbe, *Life*, 1947 (1834), p. 193.
[31.] Powell, 2004, p. 266.

> Something of Impropriety was hinted by her as we proceeded
> & I then might have convinced myself as I did the Lady that
> I was in my 58th year & this with my Profession & I cannot
> tell what more, put an End to all Scruples of this kind: so we
> wrote on & shall I say the very Truth? I must! Let me whisper
> then, that I soon began to dream Dreams of unseasonable
> Happiness. I fancied this Nymph unlike her Sister Nymphs,
> one who wd forget my Time of Life & loose the thought of
> Gravity & Coldness in the Strength & Ardour of the Language
> I insensibly adopted.[32]

It did not prove so, of course – not at that time, nor place. Crabbe was not to enjoy the ultimate happiness of a close companion – something also denied him for much of his marriage. But he was still writing. By 1817–18, he was engaged on what was to be the last of his published works, eventually printed as *Tales of the Hall* by John Murray in 1819.

He would work mainly at night, with a glass of weak spirits by his side, indulging in snuff. His son describes the library in words that falter with the attempt to conjure its disarray: a 'scene of unparalleled confusion – windows rattling, paint in great request, books in every direction but the right – the table – but no, I cannot find terms to describe it".[33]

Trowbridge: A few Sundays more

Crabbe's late-night exertions in his study led, in June 1819, to the publication of *Tales of the Hall* – the last major work of his lifetime. He received the handsome sum of £3,000 from publisher John Murray. Friends urged him immediately to take the bills to show his sons or they would not believe his good luck. The deal proved rather less fortuitous for the publisher: 'it was a matter of common knowledge in the literary world of Crabbe's day that John Murray did not on this occasion make a very prudent bargain,' observes Alfred Ainger, 'and that in fact he lost heavily by his venture'.[34]

[32.] Letter to Elizabeth Charter, 5 May 1815. See Crabbe, *Letters*, 1985, p. 172.
[33.] Crabbe, *Life*, 1947 (1834), p. 229.
[34.] Ainger, 1903, p. 159.

Endings and Beginnings

The publisher was banking on success similar to that of *The Borough* (1810), which had run to six editions in six years, and *Tales* (1812), five editions in two years. But poetic tastes had altered in the seven years since that last publication, and the literary marketplace was crowded.

Byron had produced the four cantos of *Childe Harold* between 1812 and 1818, and other poems 'rich in splendid rhetoric and a lyric versatility far beyond Crabbe's reach'.[35] Wordsworth's two volumes of *Poems*, published in 1815, were attracting his own public. Keats's first book, *Poems*, appeared in March 1817, and *Endymion* in 1818 (with more to follow the year after the publication of *Tales of the Hall*), and Sir Walter Scott released five or six of his best novels in these years. Ainger speculates: 'By the side of this fascinating prose, and still more fascinating metrical versatility, Crabbe's resolute and plodding couplets might often seem tame and wearisome.'[36] A somewhat damning assessment – but without doubt, the rhyming couplet was falling out of fashion.

There was also Crabbe's uncompromising and sometimes dark subject matter – this too remained a constant. Ainger continues: 'the reader would not make much progress in these volumes without discovering that the depressing incidents of life, its disasters and distresses, were still Crabbe's prevailing theme'.[37] One contemporary critic of *Tales of the Hall* remarked upon the 'deeply tragical and, at the same time, revolting' story of Ruth, in reference to the tale of a young woman who drowns herself to escape a lecherous preacher.[38] Another critic, at least, noted the preponderance of romantic stories in the collection – 'and the various feelings, bad and good (not always the latter), detailed in connection with the passion of love'.[39]

There were favourable appraisals: Francis Jeffrey, by now a seasoned Crabbe commentator, wrote in *The Edinburgh Review* in July 1819, calling the poet 'this great writer', and adding that he was 'the greatest *mannerist*, perhaps, of all living poets', notwithstanding the 'eternal full-lengths of low and worthless characters' Crabbe had once again depicted. 'Mr Crabbe, accordingly, has other gifts;' he maintained, 'and those are not less peculiar or less strongly marked than the blemishes

---

[35]. Ibid, p. 160.
[36]. Ibid.
[37]. Ainger, 1903, p. 160–61.
[38]. Unsigned review in *The Eclectic Review*, Vol. 13 (February, 1820): p. 122. Cf. Huchon, 1907, p. 429.
[39]. Unsigned review in *The Christian Observer*, Vol. 18 (October 1819): p. 665.

with which they contrasted.' These included 'an unrivalled and an almost magical power of observation' and 'an anatomy of character and feeling not less exquisite and searching', as well as 'an occasional touch of matchless tenderness' and a 'deep and dreadful pathetic, interspersed by fits, and strangely interwoven with the most minute and humble of details'. Crabbe, he observed with particular insight, 'seems to have become more amorous as he grows older'.[40]

The reviewer for *The British Critic* was less sanguine. In a sustained attack in September that year, the anonymous writer remarked: 'We think that he has never yet written so unequally; and we fear we may add never with so great a preponderance of his peculiar faults.'

Chief among these faults was the unremitting concentration on base detail for which Crabbe was by then renowned. 'It is not that we wish every thing to be elevated,' the critic insisted, 'but that we wish nothing to be mean [...] with Mr. Crabbe, not a wart, a wrinkle, or a freckle, escapes faithful notice; nay, sometimes, we are convinced, that he resents the rubicundity of a nose, and distorts the obliquity of an eye'.[41]

To give the final word to a more recent critic, writing in a more measured tone in the 1930s, F.R. Leavis hailed *Tales of the Hall* a 'living classic, because it is in this work that [Crabbe] develops to the full his peculiarly eighteenth-century strength. His strength is that of a novelist and of an eighteenth-century poet who is positively in sympathy with the Augustan tradition.'[42]

Crabbe himself described his new volume – 'probably (most probably) the last work I shall publish' – in these words:

> Though a village is the scene of meeting between my two principal characters, and gives occasion to other characters and relations in general, yet I no more describe the manners of village inhabitants. My people are of superior classes, though not the most elevated; and, with a few exceptions are of educated and cultivated minds and habits.[43]

---

[40] Francis Jeffrey, unsigned review in *The Edinburgh Review*, Vol. 32, No. 63 (July 1819): p. 119.

[41] Unsigned review in *The British Critic*, Vol. 12 (September 1819): p. 289.

[42] F.R. Leavis, *Revaluation: Tradition and Development in English Poetry* (London: Chatto and Windus, 1936), p. 125.

[43] Letter to Mary Leadbeater, October 1817. Quoted in Ainger, 1903, p. 163.

His reputation as a writer was now well established – both positively and negatively. In his subject matter he had moved from the 'bold, artful, surly, savage race' of *The Village* to the scenario of two long-lost half brothers, George and Richard, who are reunited and living in 'The Hall', where they relate tales to each other over port wine. The brothers' comfortable seclusion reflects a shift, culturally, from the lowly existences of Crabbe's village inhabitants, as well as recalling his own geographic and social move from the raw coastal community of Aldeburgh and Slaughden to the gentler climes of Wiltshire and upper echelons of society.

The Hall which constitutes the poem's overarching setting has been constructed out of a smaller farmhouse through additions and alterations, not unlike John Tovell's house, Ducking Hall, in Parham – and similarly has a moat.

> *It was an ancient, venerable hall,*
> *And once surrounded by a moat and wall;*
> *A part was added by a squire of taste,*
> *Who, while unvalued acres ran to waste,*
> *Made spacious rooms, whence he could look about,*
> *And mark improvements as they rose without:*
> *He fill'd the moat, he took the wall away,*
> *He thinn'd the park, and bade the view be gay:*[44]

But the poem's stories, as much as their settings, draw upon Crabbe's earlier life in Suffolk. 'Boys at School' describes a boy who liked art but had little talent. His ambitions were thwarted and he died, a destitute man, in a workhouse. The story of unfulfilled ambition is close to that of Crabbe's brother-in-law, James Elmy, who likewise died as a young man – possibly as early as 1788 – after failing in his attempt to become an artist. 'At length he pined away, a victim to disappointment and melancholy', recounts Crabbe's son in a footnote to his father's *Poetical Works*, 'and the last effort of his sinking strength was to commit all his drawings to the flames.'[45]

[44.] 'The Hall', Book I, *Tales of the Hall*. See Crabbe, *Poetical Works*, p. 342. Cf. The younger Crabbe's recollection of John Tovell's property: 'His house was large, and the surrounding moat, the rookery, the ancient dovecot, and the well-stored fishponds, were such as might have suited a gentleman's seat of some consequence;'

[45.] Crabbe, 1834, Vol. VI, p. 53, n. 1.

In 'The Natural Death of Love', the rector of the parish is thought to be a portrait of Crabbe himself, as he appeared to his dissenting parishioners at Muston ('"A moral teacher!" some, contemptuous, cried; / He smiled, but nothing of the fact denied, / Nor save by his fair life, to charge so strong replied.')[46]

And in 'Adventures of Richard', the backstory of one of the brothers opens with his residing with his mother near a small seaport – reliving Crabbe's own memories of the Aldeburgh seascape:

> *'I loved to stop at every creek and bay*
> *Made by the river in its winding way,*
> *And call to memory – not by marks they bare,*
> *But by the thoughts that were created there.*
> *Pleasant it was to view the sea-gulls strive*
> *Against the storm, or in the ocean dive,*
> *With eager scream, or when they dropping gave*
> *Their closing wings to sail upon the wave:*
> *Then as the winds and waters raged around,*
> *And breaking billows mix'd their deafening sound,*
> *They on the rolling deep securely hung,*
> *And calmly rode the restless waves among.*
> *Nor pleased it less around me to behold,*
> *Far up the beach, the yesty sea-foam roll'd;*
> *Or from the shore upborn, to see on high,*
> *Its frothy flakes in wilde confusion fly:*
> *While the salt spray that clashing billows form,*
> *Gave to the taste a feeling of the storm.'*[47]

Tales of the Hall was the last work to be published in Crabbe's lifetime. It failed to sell out in its first edition; John Murray lost out to the tune of £2,500 – a substantial loss. The commercial disappointment marked a change of pace in Crabbe's life – and perhaps a shift in perspective. In his final years, he focused chiefly on his parishioners and work as a clergyman, visiting London less frequently and retreating from the social whirlwind he had in recent years enjoyed. His son recounts:

---

[46] 'The Natural Death of Love', Book XIV, *Tales of the Hall*. See Crabbe, *Poetical Works,* 1932, pp. 437–38. See also p. 136 above.

[47] 'Adventures of Richard', Book IV, *Tales of the Hall*. See Crabbe, *Poetical Works,* 1932, p. 359.

Endings and Beginnings

> Advancing age, failing health, the tortures of tic douloureux [neuralgia], with which he began to be afflicted about 1820, and, I may add, the increasing earnestness of his devotional feelings, rendered him, in his closing years, less and less anxious to mingle much in the scenes of gaiety and fashion.[48]

His gregarious days behind him, Crabbe continued to officiate at church until the last two Sundays before he died. And in 1825, at the age of seventy-one, he became a magistrate. But despite this contraction of his focus towards clerical and civic duties, he did continue to meet with leading writers. It was in 1822, the last of his very active seasons in London, that he made the trip to meet Sir Walter Scott in Edinburgh. And in 1828, he encountered fellow poets William Wordsworth and Robert Southey in London.

At Trowbridge, Crabbe's younger son, John, served as his father's curate and lived with him in the rectory. Crabbe would also regularly visit his other clergyman son George, later the biographer, and his family at nearby Pucklechurch. On these visits, he would hunt in the mornings for fossils, even in the roughest weather, and come back with his assorted geological finds – along with any uncommon weeds. His son touchingly recalls: 'The dirty fossils were left in our best bed-room, to the great diversion of the female part of the family; the herbs stuck in the borders, among my choice flowers, that he might see them when he came again. I never displaced one of them.'[49]

In January 1831, the year before his death, Crabbe was thinking about one more visit to Suffolk. He wrote that 'A long Journey, as that would be into Suffolk, I contemplate with mixed feelings of Hope & Apprehendsion.' Partly this was down to his ailing health and the predictable ordeal of a long journey; but it seems that his deeper feelings about Aldeburgh and Suffolk remained contradictory:

> Yet I should rejoice to re-visit Beccles where Every One is kind to me & where every Object I view has the Appearance of Friendship & Welcome. Beccles is the Home of past Years & I could not walk through its Streets as a Stranger: It is not so at Aldborough; there a Sadness mixes with all I see or hear: Not

---

[48.] Crabbe, *Life*, 1947 (1834), p. 237.
[49.] Ibid, p. 270.

a Man is living whom I knew in my early portion of Life, my Contemporaries are gone and their Successors are unknown to me and I to them.[50]

Crabbe seems to have been thinking back to his visit to Aldeburgh in June 1826, following the death of his brother-in-law, Thomas Sparkes. He wrote on that occasion of a walk with his niece 'one Evening to Thorpe at low water', during which 'the Haven actually broke through in two places before our return, but so that we could easily step over with wetted feet only'.[51]

In his letter of 1831, he recollected a similar walk with his niece through a melancholic and estranged version of Aldeburgh. However, by his own account, Crabbe did happen to pass an old man who – as his niece realised – had known and played with Crabbe when the two of them were boys ('he looks as if he wanted to tell you so', she told her uncle). Crabbe recorded afterwards: 'Of course, I stopped in my Way & Zekiel Thorpe and I became once more Acquainted.'[52] His claim that 'Not a man is living whom I knew in my early portion of Life', then, was not fully accurate – more a profession of his state of mind. Crabbe's walk in Aldeburgh, probably his last, was a sad, introspective moment – not even a chance meeting with an old associate could leaven his sense of alienation from the old place.

The *tic douloureux*, or neuralgia, from which he suffered by now, was a more persistent source of distress. It meant that he was at times in severe pain when taking a church service, being obliged to 'stop and press his hand hard to his face, and then his pale countenance became flushed'. His son records: 'he would say, "Well! – one Sunday more;", or, "a few Sundays more, but not many."'[53] Yet in November 1831, only weeks before he died, he visited his son George at Pucklechurch and preached at both his churches, where he seemed so strong and powerful that his son was 'much comforted with the indications of a long,

---

[50.] Letter to William Henchman Crowfoot, 19 January 1831. See Crabbe, *Letters*, 1985, p. 373. Crowfoot was a relative of his son John's wife.

[51.] Letter to George Crabbe Jr., 28 June 1826. See Crabbe, *Letters*, 1985, p. 333. On this visit, Crabbe also sponsored an old friend – John Wilson Croker – as the Tory candidate in the elections then taking place.

[52.] Letter to William Henchman Crowfoot, 19 January 1831. See Crabbe, *Letters*, 1985, p. 373.

[53.] Crabbe, *Life*, 1947 (1834), p. 271.

protracted decline', and was inspired to declare: 'Why, Sir, I will venture a good sum that you will be assisting me ten years hence.' 'Ten weeks' was Crabbe's phlegmatic answer.[54] It was unnervingly accurate.

The end was sudden and swift. On 29 January 1832, his son George received a letter from his younger brother, John, saying that their father had 'caught a sharp cold, accompanied with oppression in the chest and pain in the forehead'. He had been bled; but the very next morning, John sent a chaise to collect his brother and bring him to Trowbridge, as 'all hope of recovery was already over'.[55]

Over the course of a few days, Crabbe declined physically although not mentally: 'He knew there was no chance of his recovery, and yet he talked at intervals of his death, and of certain consequent arrangements with a strong complacent voice; and bade us all adieu without the least faltering of the tongue or moisture of the eye.'[56] During the night of 2 February, the brothers sat in turn at their father's bedside. George heard him say: 'All is well at last!'[57]

Crabbe's younger son John was with him when he died at seven o'clock on the morning of 3 February 1832, aged seventy-seven. News of his death reverberated around the town. 'The shutters of the shops in the town were half closed, as soon as his death was known,' recalls his biographer son.

> On the day of his funeral, ninety-two of the principal inhabitants, including all the dissenting ministers, assembling of their own accord in the school-room, followed him to the grave. The shops on this day were again closed; the streets crowded; the three galleries and the organ loft were hung with black cloth, as well as the pulpit and chancel. The choir was in mourning – the other inhabitants of the town were in their seats and in mourning – the church was full – the effect appalling.

[54.] Crabbe, *Life*, 1947 (1834), p. 278.

[55.] Ibid, p. 279.

[56.] Ibid, pp. 279–80.

[57.] Ibid, p. 282.

Figure 18. Monument to George Crabbe, St James's Church, Trowbridge

The master of the Free and Sunday school at Trowbridge, a Mr Nightingale, gave an address on the Sunday after the funeral, which contained the following account: '"Poor Mr Crabbe," said a little girl, the other day very simply, "poor Mr Crabbe will never go up in the pulpit any more with his white head."'[58]

[58.] Ibid, pp. 282–83.

Endings and Beginnings

Crabbe was buried in the sanctuary of his church, St James, Trowbridge – a striking spired building dating from the fifteenth century and now Grade One listed. The chancel bears on its north wall a marble memorial to the poet, commissioned by Crabbe's friends and parishioners from the neoclassical sculptor Edward Hodges Baily (who later created the statue of Nelson for the top of Nelson's column). It consists of a relief carving depicting the poet on his deathbed, clutching a book to his chest and spirited along – or watched over – by four muse-like angels. A large goblet stands on a table close to his feet, the cup of Christ, but an apt reminder too of the fortifying glass that Crabbe had kept by his writing desk. The inscription begins:

> Born in humble life, he made himself what he was; breaking through the obscurity of his birth by the force of his genius; yet he never ceased to feel for the less fortunate; entering (as his works can testify) into the sorrow and deprivations of the poorest of his parishioners.

* * *

The poet of the poor had died far away from the place of his birth and early life – from Aldeburgh and Suffolk – but those places had always remained with him, enduring and evolving through his writing.

He long had an ambivalent relationship with the locality, and yet it was this ambivalence, as E.M. Forster described in his 1948 lecture at the Aldeburgh Festival, that provided a vital catalyst – playing an essential part in the creation of 'Peter Grimes' and other works:

> It was not a straight-forward antipathy. It was connected with a profound attraction. He might leave Aldeburgh with his body, but he never emigrated spiritually; here on the plane of creation was his home, and he could not have found a better one. This Borough made him a poet, through it he understood Suffolk, and through East Anglia he approached England. He remains here, however far he seems pleased to travel, whatever he says to the contrary.
>
> [...] His best work describes the place directly – The Village, The Parish Register, The Borough – and its atmosphere follows him when he attempts other themes.[59]

[59.] Forster, 1972 (1948), p. 168.

That atmosphere, of course, went on to inspire other artists and writers; its reverberation through later imaginations – and the kind of hold it still exercises – is well summed up by Constantin Cavafy's 1924 poem about Alexandria, 'The City':

> *You won't find a new country, won't find another shore.*
> *This city will always pursue you.*
> *You'll walk the same streets, grow old*
> *In the same neighbourhoods, turn gray in these same houses.*
> *You'll always end up in this city.*[60]

But Crabbe should have the final word. On a visit to Aldeburgh in October 1823 – one of his last – he penned some lines in his notebook that evoked his feelings on returning to what he still called home, despite the changes the town had undergone. The lines bear witness to his undying emotional connection with Aldeburgh. And they stand, after a lifelong relationship, as an informal valedictory to the coastal town – to the place and his time there.

> *Thus once again, my native place, I come*
> *Thee to salute – my earliest, latest home:*
> *Much are we alter'd both, but I behold*
> *In thee a youth renewed – whilst I am old.*
> *The works of man from dying we may save*
> *But man himself moves onward to the grave.*[61]

---

[60] Forster had met the Greek poet in Alexandria during the First World War and in 1923 was instrumental in introducing him to a British literary public, just as he went on years later to 'introduce' Crabbe to Britten. In a monograph on the Greek poet published in 1923, Forster wrote of Cavafy's moods as 'intensely subjective; scenery, cities and legends all re-emerge in terms of the mind.' See Forster, 1923, p, 247. Cf. Edmund Blunden's concept of the 'psychological landscape': see Introduction.

[61] Crabbe, *Life*, 1947 (1834), p. 251.

Postscript

On the wall in my house in Aldeburgh is a large portrait. It is of my parents, Bettina and Matthew Gibb – and was painted by my youngest son, Patrick, from a photograph dating from the 1940s. It seems fitting that it surveys the main room and that my parents are a presence here.

It was my parents, after all, who introduced our family to Aldeburgh in the mid 1960s, some six decades ago. They brought us here by chance on a family summer holiday and fell in love with the place. So began a lifelong relationship with this little understated town.

They were not part of the established communities of sailors or golfers; they did not join clubs or societies – they did not even attend the concerts or the Festival with any great regularity. What they loved was more commonplace – walking their golden Labrador on the marshes; the proximity of the shops and the beach; the cinema; quiet evenings reading.

The shops over the years would change – in my parents' time, sacks of flour would be hoisted each night into the side wall of what was Smith's Bakery (now the Two Magpies) for the baking of bread. But in essence, the High Street has remained much the same. My mother would, as I do now, collect her newspaper from Baggott & Son; my father rummage for new and doubtless superfluous screws in the hardware store. They would enthuse about the carnival, the lantern procession, the often-glorious weather with its luminous mistiness, and the clear starry nights.

They were fortunate in being able to buy a house in West Lane, the middle set of steps leading up from the High Street to the Terrace. Some five years later, they moved to Hartington Road, set back a minute or two from the shops, at the top of Choppings Hill.

It was here that my parents came, week in, week out, to spend every weekend and holidays, escaping the daily grind of London and my father's work as a solicitor; here, too, that we, as a family, brought our newly born children – in the case of my three sons, each within a month of birth. Over the decades, the house and Aldeburgh have been the constant in our lives, through teenage years, marriages, children, job changes, house moves and deaths.

In the early years, I went to Norwich to read English at the University of East Anglia, and I came with our university choir to perform occasionally at Snape Maltings. Later, when I had first met my husband, Joe, it was to Aldeburgh that I brought him for a day trip. After he died at the end of 2009, I came here often – it was a sanctuary, always sustaining, reviving, and above all peaceful.

My parents' ashes are interred in the church's Lawn Cemetery, along with those of my husband and sister – you can see the sea, as you stand there, looking out in one direction – and in the other, the reassuring, ancient presence of the church of St Peter and St Paul.

Aldeburgh has meant different things at different times. Its appeal shifted from dinghy sailing in our teenage years to the pleasures of the pebble beach, boating pond and the carnival when the children were small. And there were always the marshes, especially with the advent of a trio of Labradors and other dogs (a total of eight across the family), the Festival, concerts, restaurants, pubs, the bookshop and the church. Family are here still: my brother comes each year; my brother-in-law lives in Sternfield, his mother in Aldeburgh.

You can't be in Aldeburgh and not be aware of Benjamin Britten – whether from Festival performances, the magnificent John Piper stained glass memorial window, the Red House where Britten and Pears lived, or from Maggi Hambling's *Scallop*. But unless you know the story of Peter Grimes, you may not know of George Crabbe.

You might come across the street named after him, of course – if only to visit the Cross Keys pub – or discover his marble bust in a corner of the church. And so, like Britten some eighty years ago in that bookshop in California, you might – as I did – begin a journey, taking you below the surface layers of this place to the poetry beneath.

Bibliography

Ainger, Alfred. 1903. *English Men of Letters: Crabbe*. London: Macmillan

Auden, W.H. 2015. *The Complete Works of W.H. Auden: Prose, Volume V, 1963–1968*. Edited by Edward Mendelson. Princeton: Princeton University Press

Blackburne, Neville. 1972. *The Restless Ocean: The Story of George Crabbe, the Aldeburgh Poet, 1754–1832*. Lavenham: Terence Dalton

Blunden, Edmund. 1947. 'Father and Son.' In George Crabbe, *The Life of George Crabbe by his Son*. London: Cresset Press, pp. vii-xxv

Blythe, Ronald. 1999. *Talking About John Clare*. Nottingham: Trent Editions

———. 2013. *The Time by the Sea: Aldeburgh, 1955–1958*. London: Faber and Faber

Britten, Benjamin. 1945. Introduction to Sadler's Wells Opera Guide, *Peter Grimes*. London: John Lane; The Bodley Head, pp. 7–8

———. 1964. *On Receiving the First Aspen Award: A Speech*. London: Faber and Faber

Britten, Benjamin, and Slater, Montagu. 1961. *Peter Grimes: An Opera in Three Acts and a Prologue*. London: Boosey & Hawkes (originally published 1945)

Britten, Beth. 1986. *My Brother Benjamin*. Bourne End: The Kensal Press

Carpenter, Humphrey. 1992. *Benjamin Britten: A Biography*. London: Faber and Faber

Chesterton, G.K. 2007. *Tremendous Trifles*. Mineola, NY: Dover Publications (originally published 1909)

Crabbe, George [Sr.]. 1816. 'Biographical Account of George Crabbe.' *New Monthly Magazine*, Vol. 4, January: pp. 511–17

———. 1932. *The Poetical Works of George Crabbe*. Edited by A.J. Carlyle and R.M. Carlyle. London: Oxford University Press; Humphrey Milford

———. 1985. *Selected Letters and Journals of George Crabbe*. Edited by Thomas C. Faulkner. Oxford: Clarendon Press

———. 2015. *Selected Poems*. Edited by Gavin Edwards. London: Penguin Classics

Crabbe, George [Jr.]. 1834. *The Poetical Works of the Rev. George Crabbe, with his Letters and Journals, and Life by his Son. Volume VI.* Edited by George Crabbe. London: John Murray

——. 1932. *The Life of George Crabbe by his Son.* London: Oxford University Press; Humphrey Milford (originally published 1834)

——. 1947. *The Life of George Crabbe by his Son.* London: Cresset Press (originally published 1834)

Cranbrook, Earl of. 1949. 'George Crabbe and Great Glemham.', *Proceedings of the Suffolk Institute of Archaeology and Natural History*, Vol. 15, No. 1: pp. 116–17

Dutt, William A. 1909. *Suffolk.* Cambridge: Cambridge University Press

Fairhall, David. 2013. *East Anglian Shores.* London: Adlard Coles Nautical (originally published 1988)

Finlayson, Iain. 1993. *Tangier: City of the Dream.* London: Flamingo

Forster, Edward Morgan. 1923. *Pharos and Pharillon.* London: Hogarth Press

——. 'Introduction.' In George Crabbe, *The Life of George Crabbe by his Son.* London: Oxford University Press, pp. vii-xix.

——. 1941. 'George Crabbe: The Poet and the Man.' *The Listener*, Vol. 25, No. 646, 29 May: pp. 769–70 [text of a broadcast talk, BBC Overseas Service, 17 May 1941]

——. 1948. 'George Crabbe and Peter Grimes.' A lecture given at the Aldeburgh Festival, 7 June 1948. Printed in E.M. Forster, *Two Cheers for Democracy.* London: Edward Arnold, 1972, pp. 166–80 (originally published 1951)

Hambling, Maggi. 2010. *The Aldeburgh Scallop.* Framlingham: Full Circle Editions

Hartley, Nigel. 2014. 'Introduction.' In *Aldeburgh Parish Church, St Peter and St Paul: A Guide.* Leiston: Leiston Press, p. 5

Hayter, Alethea. 1968. *Opium and the Romantic Imagination.* Berkeley: University of California Press

Herz, Judith. 1988. *The Short Narratives of E.M. Forster.* London: Macmillan

Hoare, Sarah, and Hannah Hoare. 1911. *Memoirs of Samuel Hoare by his Daughter Sarah and his Widow Hannah.* London: Headley Brothers

Hollinghurst, Alan, 2004. 'Claws out for Crabbe.' *The Guardian*, 24 April: p. 14

Huchon, René. 1907. *George Crabbe and his Times, 1754–1832.* Translated by Frederick Clarke. London: John Murray

Jeffrey, Francis. 1808. 'Poems. By the Reverend George Crabbe.' *The Edinburgh Review*, Vol. 12, No. 23, April: pp. 131–51

——. 1810. 'The Borough: A Poem, in Twenty-four Letters.' *The Edinburgh Review*, Vol. 16, No. 31, April: pp. 30–55

——. 1812. 'Tales: By the Reverend George Crabbe.' *The Edinburgh Review*, Vol. 20, No. 40, November: pp. 277–305

Kebbel, Thomas Edward. 1888. *Life of George Crabbe.* London: Walter Scott

Bibliography

Kirby, John. 1839. *A Topographical and Historical Description of the County of Suffolk*. Woodbridge: J. Munro

Lange, Helen, 2011. 'Thomas Hardy and George Crabbe.' *The Hardy Society Journal*, Vol.7, No. 2, Summer: pp. 34–50

Leavis, Frank Raymond. 1936. *Revaluation: Tradition and Development in English Poetry*. London: Chatto and Windus

McGann, Jerome. 1989. 'George Crabbe: Poetry and Truth.' *London Review of Books*, Vol. 11, No. 6, 16 March: pp. 16–17

Mitchell, Donald, and Reed, Philip, eds. 1991a. *Letters from a Life: Selected Letters and Diaries of Benjamin Britten, 1913–1976, Volume One, 1923–39*. London: Faber and Faber

Mitchell, Donald, and Reed, Philip, eds. 1991b. *Letters from a Life: Selected Letters and Diaries of Benjamin Britten, 1913–1976, Volume Two, 1939–45*. London: Faber and Faber

Mitford, John. 1834. 'Life of the Poet Crabbe.' *The Gentleman's Magazine*, new series, Vol. 1, March: pp. 253–64

Morrison, Blake. 2013. 'The Man behind Benjamin Britten'. *The Guardian*. 14 June

———. 2015. *Shingle Street*. London: Chatto and Windus

Morrison, Richard. 2013. 'Peter Grimes at Aldeburgh Beach, Suffolk.' *The Times*, 19 June

Neville, Sylas. 1950. *Diary, 1767–1788*. Edited by Basil Conzens-Hardy. London: Oxford University Press

Peacock, Markham L. 1950. *The Critical Opinions of William Wordsworth*. Baltimore: Johns Hopkins University Press

Pevsner, Nikolaus. 1974. *The Buildings of England: Suffolk*. 2nd edition, revised by Enid Radcliffe. London: Penguin Books

Pollard, Arthur, ed. 1972. *Crabbe: The Critical Heritage*. London: Routledge & Kegan Paul

Powell, Neil. 2004. *George Crabbe: An English Life, 1754–1832*. London: Pimlico

White, Eric Walter. 1970. *Benjamin Britten: His Life and Operas*. London: Faber and Faber; Boosey & Hawkes

Whitehead, Frank. 1995. *George Crabbe: A Reappraisal*. Selinsgrove: Susquehanna University Press

Winborn, Colin, 2004. *The Literary Economy of Jane Austen and George Crabbe*. Aldershot; Burlington, VT: Ashgate

Film and video

Palmer, Tony, dir. 1979. *A Time There Was*

Index

Note: *italicised* page references indicate illustrations; the suffix 'n' indicates a note.

abolitionism 100, 142, 143
Ainger, Alfred 65–6, 70–1, 96, 97, 108, 111, 119, 130, 150, 151
Albery, Tim 111
Aldeburgh beach 6, 13, 14, 21, 25, 26, *35*, 72, 75–6, 97, 123, 129
   Britten on *3*, 104, 111
   Peter Grimes (Britten) performed on 6, *105*, 111–14, 116
   Scallop (sculpture) on *3*, 103–6, *105*
Aldeburgh Festival 3, 10, 14, 34, 159, 162
Aldeburgh, Suffolk 1–6, *3*, 7, 12–28, *15*, *23*, *24*, 32–9, *35*, *105*, 161–2
   bookshop 14–16, 162
   Britten in *3*, 8, 104, 111
   Crabbe revisits 71–2, 108, 134–5, 155–6, 160
   Crabbe's curacy at 4–5, 61–8, 83–6, 87
   Crabbe's feelings towards 4–5, 16–17, 36–7, 134–5, 155–6, 159
   Crabbe's poems inspired by 1, 4–5, 17, 36–7, 106–7, 119, 154, 159
   Crabbe's standing in 4–5, 61–2, 64–5, 66, 99
   Crabbe Street 14–16, 22–3
   Crabbe surgeon-apothecary at 4–5, 37–8, 39, 40–1, 48, 55, 59, 62, 65–6, 91–2, 107, 122
   Leech Pond 2, 33–4, 41
   Marsh Hill 33, 34
   Moot Hall 1, 14, *15*, 22–3, 37
   Red House 8, 162
   workhouse/poorhouse 40–1, 120, 122
   see also Slaughden Quay; St Peter and St Paul church, Aldeburgh
Alde estuary 3, 4, 10, 11–12, 21, 97, 114, 123
Alde, river 10, 16, 25, 26, *35*, 82, 83
Alexandria 34n77, 160
Allington, Lincolnshire 73, 82
America 2, 7–10, 57, 98, 146
anatomy 38, 40
Auden, W.H. 7, 8n7

Baily, Edward Hodges 159
Ballitore, Ireland 118, 146
Barton, Bernard 22
Bath, Somerset 140, 149
Beaconsfield, Buckinghamshire 59–60
Beccles, Suffolk 45, 47–8, 59, 69, 94, 119, 155
Belvoir Castle, Leicestershire 68, 70, 76, 99, 101
Benett, John 136
Benhall, Suffolk 47
Bennett, John 107
Bessborough, Henrietta ('Harriet'), Countess 141
Blunden, Edmund 5, 117, 121
Blythburgh, Suffolk 64

Blythe, Ronald 3, 17, 30–1
The Borough (Crabbe) 5, 24, 36–7, 86, 103, 106–11, 118–21, 123–5, 126, 128, 131, 151, 159
  preface 110, 114–15, 119, 120, 127n70, 128
  reception 2, 11, 108–11, 117–18, 120
  'Abel Keene' 106–7, 124–5
  'The Alms-House And Trustees' 118–19
  'Amusements' 39n96
  'Ellen Orford' 121
  'General Description' 72
  'The Hospital and Governors' 50
  'The Parish-Clerk' 106–7, 123
  'The Poor and their Dwellings' 120
  'Schools' 20, 27, 29
  see also 'Peter Grimes' (Crabbe)
Boudicca, Queen 82–3
Bowles, Reverend William Lisle 141
Bowood House, Wiltshire 141
The British Critic 152
Britten, Alan 116
Britten, Benjamin 3, 12, 14, 34n77, 111
  Aldeburgh beach, on 3, 104, 111
  Aldeburgh, commemorated in 19, 66, 103–6, *105*, 111–14, 162
  Aldeburgh, resides in 8, 34n77, 104, 106, 111, 162
  in America 2, 7–10
  centenary of 111–14
  childhood 7, 10, 113
  discovers Crabbe 2, 7–12, *9*, 117, 160n60
  John Piper stained glass windows 19, 66, 162
  Peter Grimes 2, 6, 10, 103, 104, *105*, 111–16, 117, 121
  'Sea Interludes' 104
  at Snape 2, 10
  Suffolk, nostalgia for 2, 8, 10, 12
Britten Pears Arts 8n5
Brougham, Henry 143
Brown, Tom 107
Bulman, Job *15*
Bungay Grammar School (now Bungay High School) 28
Burcham, Mrs 52–3
Burke, Edmund 2, 36, 38, 56–61, 66, 68, 78, 91, 94, 100, 118, 127, 139, 141, 146

Burns, Robert 52
Byron, Reverend Henry 134
Byron, Lord 92, 134, 141, 143, 151

California 2, 7–8, 10
Cambridge University 60, 76, 83–6, 127, 128
Campbell, Thomas 143
Canning, George 143
Cartwright, Dr Edmund Sr. 75, 101
Cartwright, Edmund Jr. 12n15, 75–6, 77, 79–80, 101
Catholics/Catholicism 57, 98
Cavafy, Constantin 160
Charter, Elizabeth 106, 143n14, 147, 149–50
Chatterton, Thomas 52
Chesterton, G.K. 20
Churchill, Charles 52
Clark, Dr Nicholas 8n5
Claudius, Emperor 82–3
Clements, Andrew 112
Cliff House, Cromer, Norfolk 143
Clubbe, Dr 93
coffee houses 53, 140
Colchester, Essex 83
Coleridge, Samuel Taylor 92, 96–7, 109
Cornwall 147
Cowper, William 52
Crabbe, Edmund (Crabbe's son) 77
Crabbe, George, general
  appearance 17, *18*, *138*, 139, 142
  botanical interests 5, 38–9, 40, 50, 72, 73, 75–6, 81, 89, 91, 128, 144, 155
  bust of 17–19, *18*, 66
  character 70–1, 77, 86, 88, 92, 99–100, 136, 139–40, 141, 144, 145, 155
  classical learning 29, 53, 61, 91
  entomological interests 5, 38, 39, 81, 82
  faith 41–2, 60–1, 89–91, 133, 155
  father, relationship with 27–8, 34, 37, 63–4, 72, 107–8, 131
  fossil-hunting 144, 155
  opium (laudanum), use of 92–7
  political allegiances 78, 98–102, 136
  poor, concern for the 40–1, 71, 102, 109–10, 120–3, 132, 159
  walking, enjoyment of 29, 39, 40, 48, 75–6, 82, 86, 128
  women, dealings with 44, 145–50

Index

Crabbe, George, church career 2, 29, 62, 70–1, 72, 82, 87–92, 101
  Aldeburgh, curate at 4–5, 61–8, 83–6, 87
  Allington benefice 73, 82
  Dorset livings 68n77, 73
  Duke of Rutland at Belvoir Castle, chaplain to 68, 69–70, 76, 99, 101
  Great Glemham, curate at 75, 78, *79*, 86, 87, 89
  'Lambeth degree' 73
  Muston, rector of 73–4, 76–7, 82, 83–6, 92–3, 94, 98–9, 108, 119, 125–6, 128, 132–4, 136, 154
  ordination 61
  sermons 87–8, 92
  Stathern, curate at 70–3, 92
  Sweffling, curate at 74–5, 87
  theological doctrine 89, 136
  Trowbridge, vicar at 19, 134–59, *158*
Crabbe, George, life
  bicentenary celebrations 34n77, 83n36
  childhood 1–4, 12–16, 20, 21–9, *24*, 90, 106–7, 156
  children, births of 70, 76–7
  children, deaths of 70, 76–7
  courtship and engagement 43–51, 64, 90, 91, 129
  death and burial 19, 157–9, *158*
  'dissipations' 65–6, 91–2, 135
  education 27–9, 61, 74
  health, mental 94, 97, 132, 133–4, 135, 155–6
  health, physical 50, 91–4, 132, 135, 137, 155, 156–7
  Leech Pond epiphany 2, 33–4, 41
  magistrate, becomes a 101, 155
  marries Sarah Elmy 69–70
  patronage, seeks 51, 53, 55, 56–60, 94, 130
  poverty in early adulthood 41, 54, 62
  resides in Great Glemham 75, 78–82, 86, 87, 100, 127, 134
  resides in London 2, 6, 32, 34, 39–40, 42, 44, 51, 52–62, 65, 91, 92n14, 93, 98
  resides in Parham 73–80
  resides in Rendham 5, 82–6, 95, 108, 125
  resides in Trowbridge 19, 134–59
  Slaughden Quay, manual labour at 2, 3, 30, 32–3, 34, 37, 130
  surgeon-apothecary at Aldeburgh 4–5, 37–8, 39, 40–1, 48, 55, 59, 62, 65–6, 91–2, 107, 122
  surgeon-apothecary at London 39–40
  surgeon-apothecary at Wickhambrook 30
  surgeon-apothecary at Woodbridge 31, 42, 93
Crabbe, George, writings
  autobiographical sketch 31, 86, 93n21
  contemporary reception 2, 58, 69, 108–11, 118, 120, 126, 128, 151–2
  dedications 100, 102, 127–8, 142
  hiatus, 1785-1807 72–3, 86, 100, 126–7
  novels 81
  opium use 94–6
  poetry, begins to write 31–2, 53
  poetry, introduction to 27–8
  realism 1, 69, 97, 109–10, 118, 121–2, 125, 126, 146, 151–2
  English Treatise on Botany 76, 81
  'A Farewell' 43
  'Hope' 31–2
  Inebriety: A Poem in Three Parts 32
  'Infancy – a Fragment' 26–7, 106–7
  The Library 58–9, 62, 64, 93, 94, 100, 126
  'London Journal' 141
  The Newspaper 72–3, 100, 126
  'Poetic Epistles' 60–1
  'The Poet's Journal' 53–5, 60–1, 91
  Where Am I Now? 96
  The World of Dreams 96
  see also *The Borough*; *Poems*; *Tales*; *Tales of the Hall*; *The Village*
Crabbe, George (Crabbe's father) 25, 31, 41, 64, 98
  agent to Charles Long 34–6
  character 4, 36–7, 108
  churchwarden 36
  death *15*, 17, 72
  drink problem 34–7, 108
  early life 19–20
  education of his son, ensures 27–8, 56, 64, 91
  Peter Grimes, model for 36, 64, 107–8
  relationship with son 27–8, 34, 37, 63–4, 72, 107–8, 131

second marriage 72, 108
Slaughden Quay, works at 1, 2, 4, 17, 20, 30
Crabbe, George Jr. (Crabbe's son) 128, 144–5, 155, 156–7
  biography of his father 4, 6, 8, *9*, 47, *48*
  birth 70, 76
  childhood memories 72, 74, 80–91, 98
  education 74, 82, 83–6, 127
  Muston neighbourhood, curacy in 128
  Pucklechurch, curacy at 145, 155, 156–7
Crabbe, John (Crabbe's brother) 25
Crabbe, John Waldron (Crabbe's son) 22, 81, 128, 144–5, 156n50, 157
  birth 70, 76
  education 74, 82, 83–6, 127
  Muston neighbourhood, curacy in 128
  Trowbridge, father's curate at 144–5, 155
Crabbe, Mary (Crabbe's mother) *15*, 17, 26, 34, 63, 90–1
Crabbe, Mary (Crabbe's sister) *see* Sparkes, Mary (née Crabbe)
Crabbe, Rachel (Crabbe's grandmother) 19
Crabbe, Robert (Crabbe's brother) 21, 25, 64
Crabbe, Robert (Crabbe's grandfather) 19, 20
Crabbe, Sarah (Crabbe's daughter) 77
Crabbe, Sarah ('Mira') (née Elmy, Crabbe's wife) 43–51, 52–3, 81, 93, 94
  children, births of 70, 76–7
  children, deaths of 70, 76–7
  courtship and engagement 43–51, 64, 90, 91, 129
  Crabbe's letters to 53–4, 55, 60–1, 91
  death 132–3, 134–5, 145
  health, mental 77, 90, 94, 101, 110, 132–3, 145
  health, physical 50, 128
  inherits Ducking Hall 47, 73
  marries Crabbe 69–70
  parents 45, 47–8, 73
  spiritual influence on Crabbe 91
Crabbe, Sarah Susannah (Crabbe's daughter) 70, 76–7
Crabbe, William (Crabbe's brother) 25, 129

Crabbe, William (Crabbe's son) 77
Croker, John Wilson 156n51
Cromer, Norfolk 143
Crowfoot, William Henchman 156n50

dame schools 27, 74
Davies, John 76
De Quincey, Thomas 92, 93, 96
Dictionary of Irish Biography 70
Dodsley, James 59
Doncaster, South Yorkshire 101
Dorset 68n77, 73, 125
Dryden, John 54
Dublin, Ireland 57
Ducking Hall (later, Parham Lodge), Parham 45–7, *48*, 73–80, 153
Dugdale, Thomas *24*

The Eclectic Review 110
Edinburgh 142, 155
The Edinburgh Review 108–9, 118, 151–2
Elmy family 45, 47–8, 59, 73, 94
  Elmy, James 153
  see also Crabbe, Sarah ('Mira') (née Elmy, Crabbe's wife)

Farrar, Mrs John 148–9
Faulkner, Thomas C. 90
Finden, E. *48*
Finlayson, Iain 4
First World War 160n60
Fletcher, Reverend Mr 135
Forster, E.M. 11–12, 12n14, 104, 116, 160n60
  on Aldeburgh beach *3*
  at the Aldeburgh Festival 3–4, 34, 159
  on Crabbe 1, 2, 3–5, 7, 10, 11–12, 16, 17, 34, 37, 95, 114, 159
Fox, Charles James 60, 100, 127, 142
Fox-North coalition 57
Framlingham, Suffolk 44, 75
France
  French Revolution 57, 98–9
  Napoleonic Wars 97–8, 143

Gainsborough, Thomas 80
Garrard, James 66
The Gentleman's Magazine 44, 80
Gibb family 161–2

Index

Glemham Hall *see* Little Glemham Hall, Suffolk
Goadby Marwood, Leicestershire 101
Goldsmith, Oliver 52, 69, 131–2
Gordon Riots 53, 98
Gray, Thomas 52
Great Glemham, Suffolk 75, 78–82, 86, 89, 100, 127, 134
   All Saints church 78, *79*, 87
   Great Glemham Hall 78–81, 82, 127
   Great Glemham House 80
   Great Glemham Park 80
Great Yarmouth, Norfolk 76, 108
Gregories, Beaconsfield 59–60
Grey, Charles, 2nd Earl 100
Guadeloupe 47–8
The Guardian 112

Haddon, Richard 28
Hambling, Maggi 72, 104, 106
   Scallop 3, 103–6, *105*, 162
Harbord, Lady 80
Hardy, Thomas 3, 125, 135n95
Harris, John 35
Hartley, Reverend Canon Nigel 116
Hastings, Warren 57, 100
Hatchard 127
Hayter, Alethea 94
Hazlitt, William 109
Heath House, Hampstead 142–3
Hill, Susan 3
Hoare, Hannah 142–3
Hoare, Samuel 142–3
Hoare, Sarah 143, 148
Holland, Henry Richard Vassall Fox, Lord 127–8, 141–2
Holy Trinity Church, Blythburgh 64
homosexuality 106
Honduras 129
Huchon, René 6, 20, 24–5, 26, 36, 37, 41, 47, 83

Iceni 82–3
India 57
Industrial Revolution 98, 101
Ipswich, Suffolk 32, 72, 93, 98
Ireland 57, 70, 118, 146
Isherwood, Christopher 7

Jacobins 98–9
James, M.R. 3

Jeffrey, Francis 108–9, 118, 126, 128, 151–2
Johnson, Dr Samuel 52, 60, 68, 127

Keats, John 92, 151
Kelsale, Suffolk 66
Kilderbee, Dr Samuel 80

Lady's Magazine 31–2
Lady Whincup's house, Rendham 34n77, 83, *85*
Lamb, Lady Caroline 141
Lamb, Charles 22
'Lambeth degree' 73
landscape
   of Aldeburgh and environs 3–4, 6, 10, 16, 51, 104
   coastal 2, 16, 31, 117–18
   inland 44, 51, 75, 125–6
   psychological 5, 6, 11–12, 30–1, 49, 111, 116–17, 124, 160n60
Lange, Helen 125
Lansdowne family 141
laudanum (opium) 92–7
Leadbeater, Mary 118, 146–7
Leavis, F.R. 152
Leicestershire 2, 5, 6, 68, 73, 76, 82, 86, 101
Levett, William Springall 37, 44, 146
Lewis, Alethea ('Stella') (née Brereton) 90, 146
Lewis, Augustus 146
Lillywigg, Mr 76
Lincolnshire 71, 73, 82
Linnean Society 76
The Listener (magazine) 7
Little Glemham Hall, Suffolk 47, 77–8, 100, 127
Lockhart, John Gibson 142
Locri, Carl 83n36
London 68, 70
   Crabbe resides in 2, 6, 32, 34, 39–40, 42, 44, 51, 52–62, 65, 91, 92n14, 93, 98
   Crabbe revisits 132, 139, 140–1, 143–4, 154, 155
Long, Charles 34–5, 42, 61–2, 75n16, 78, 82
Lowestoft, Suffolk 10, 113
Lushington, Dr Stephen 143

Manners, Charles, 4th Duke of Rutland 68, 69, 70, 73, 78, 99, 141
Manners, John Henry, 5th Duke of Rutland 134, 135
Manners, Mary Isabella, Duchess of Rutland 69, 70, 73
Martello tower 25, 97–8
Maskill, James 37
Mayer, Elizabeth 8, 10
McGann, Jerome 109
Methodists/Methodism 65, 119n48, 133n92
Mexico 129
Miller, Elizabeth 19n27
Mill House, Snape 10
Milton, John 27–8
Mitford, John 44, 47, 80, 86
Montgomery, James 110
The Monthly Mirror 109–10
Moore, Thomas (Irish writer) 143n14
Morrison, Blake 16n18, 114n32
Morrison, Richard 112
Murray, John 150–1, 154
Muston, Leicestershire 73–4, 76–7, 82, 83–6, 92–3, 94, 98–9, 108, 119, 125–6, 128, 132–4, 136, 154

Napoleonic Wars 97–8, 143
Nelson, Horatio, 1st Viscount 159
Neville, Sylas 61
Newgate Prison 53
Norfolk 19, 28, 143
North, Dudley (was Dudley Long) 42, 47, 61–2, 75n16, 77–8, 82, 100, 127, 132
North, Lord Frederick 55, 57

Opie, Amelia 143
opium (laudanum) 92–7
Orford, Ellen (character in *The Borough*) 115–16, 121
Orford, Suffolk 10, 19–20, 25–6, 97

Page, John 31, 42
Parham, Suffolk 5, 44–7, *48*, 50–1, 64, 73, 134
  Parham Lodge (was Ducking Hall) 45–7, *48*, 73–80, 153
  St Mary the Virgin church 44, *85*, 87
patronage

Crabbe seeks 51, 53, 55, 56–60, 94, 130
Duke of Rutland 70, 73, 99–100, 130
see also Burke, Edmund; *Tales*: 'The Patron'
Peachey, General William 149
Pears, Peter *3*, 7, 8, 12, 34n77, 106, 115, 116, 117, 162
Peasenhall, Suffolk 146
Peter Grimes (Britten) 2, 6, 10, 103, 104, *105*, 111–14, 115–16, 117, 121
'Peter Grimes' (Crabbe) 2, 3–4, 10, 11–12, 14, 29, 64, 94, 103, 106–8, 110, 114–18, 159
  father's troubles, influence of 36, 64, 107–8
  wife's mental illness, influence of 94, 110
Pevsner, Nikolaus 66, 69
Pickersgill, Henry William *138*
Piper, John 19, 66, 162
Pitt, William, the Younger 70
Poems (Crabbe)
  preface 127
  The Library (revised) 126
  The Parish Register 5, 63, 86, 87, 88–9, 110, 118, 126, 127, 128, 142, 159
  Sir Eustace Grey 95–7, 126
  The Village (revised) 126
poetry
  contemporary 52, 97, 151
  Crabbe begins to write 31–2, 53
  Crabbe's introduction to 27–8
poets, contemporary 52
  Crabbe meets 141, 143, 155
  Romantic poets 2, 52, 92, 118, 126, 132, 151
Pope, Alexander 52, 141
Powell, Neil 6, 20, 30, 78, 94, 106–7, 108, 132, 149
power loom 75, 101
Powys, John Cowper 74
Pretyman, Dr George 82
psychological landscape 5, 6, 11–12, 30–1, 49, 111, 116–17, 124, 160n60
Pucklechurch, South Gloucestershire 145, 155, 156–7
Punchard, C. 32
Purcell, Henry 113

Index

Quakers 22, 142, 146

Raymond, Burham 38, 40, 122
Reform Act (1832) 100, 102, 143
Rendham, Suffolk
   Crabbe resides in 5, 82–6, 95, 108, 125
   Lady Whincup's House 34n77, 83, *85*
   St Michael's church *84*, 87
Repton, Humphrey 80n27
Revett, Mary 72
Reynolds, Sir Joshua 59, 60, 61, 68, 141
Ridout, Charlotte 148–9
Rockingham, Lord 57
Rogers, Samuel 141
Roman period 82–3
Romantic poets 2, 52, 92, 118, 126, 132, 151
Routh, Reverend Peter 69

Sadler's Wells 112–13, 115
Saxmundham, Suffolk 17, 42, 61, 75
Scott, Sir Walter 142, 143, 151, 155
Sebald, W.G. 3
Second World War 7
Seething, Norfolk 20
Shackleton, Richard 146
Shelburne, Lord 55
Shelley, Percy Bysshe 92
Slater, Enid 8
Slater, Montagu 103, 115, 117
Slaughden Quay 12–13, 19, 21–5, *23*, *35*, 97
   Crabbe's father works at 1, 2, 4, 17, 20, 30
   Crabbe works at 2, 3, 30, 32–3, 34, 37, 130
   Three Mariners public house 21, 37
Slavery Abolition Act (1833) 100, 143
Snape, Suffolk 2, 10, 14, 162
Southey, Robert 131–2, 133, 155
Sparkes, Mary (née Crabbe) 41, 50, 64, 72, 74, 134
Sparkes, Thomas 72, 74, 156
Stanfield, Clarkson 22, *24*, 47, *48*
Stathern, Leicestershire 70–3, 92, 101
Stowmarket, Suffolk 28
St Peter and St Paul church, Aldeburgh 14, 17–19, 33, *35*, 36, 72, 87, 125, 162
   bust of George Crabbe 17–19, *18*, 66

graves of Crabbe's parents *15*, 17
pulpit 66, *67*
Stradbroke, Earl of 34n77
Suffolk 82–3, 86, 106
   Britten's nostalgia for 2, 8, 10, 12
   coastal 2, 17, 19, 30–1, 39, 51, 72, 75, 104, 112
   Crabbe revisits 72, 82, 92, 93, 155
   Crabbe's feelings towards 82, 155–6
   Crabbe's poems inspired by 1, 2, 5, 17, 51, 72, 86, 106, 153, 159
   inland 5, 30–1, 44, 47, 51
   see also individual locations in
Suffolk Sandlings 75
Sweffling, Suffolk 74–5, 82, 87
Swift, Jonathan 52

Tales (Crabbe) 128–9, 131, 151
   'Edward Shore' 131
   'The Learned Boy' 131
   'The Lover's Journey' 39, 48–9, 129, 133
   'The Parting Hour' 129–30
   'The Patron' 51, 70, 130–1, 140
   'The Widow's Tale' 45–6
Tales of the Hall (Crabbe) 91, 150–4
   contemporary reception of 151–2
   'Adventures of Richard' 24n42, 29–30, 154
   'Adventures of Richard Concluded' 46–7, 49
   'Boys at School' 153
   'The Brothers' 28
   'Delay has Danger' 5
   'The Hall' 153
Tangier, Morocco 4
Taylor, Reverend J.W. 70
Tennyson, Alfred, Lord 108
Thorpeness 33, 103, 104
Thurlow, Lord Edward (Lord Chancellor) 55, 68, 73
Thurlow, Thomas (sculptor) 17, *18*
The Times 112
Tory party and politicians 78, 99–100, 101, 102, 143, 156n51
Tovell family 45, 50, 64, 74, 79
   Elizabeth Tovell 74, 79, 82
   John Tovell 44, 45, 47, 51, 73, 77
Travers, Leslie 111
Trinity College, Cambridge 60, 76

Trinity College, Dublin 57
Trowbridge, Wiltshire 1, 19, 134–59
  St James's Church *158*, 159
Turner, Reverend Richard 74–5, 108

Ufford, William de, Earl of Suffolk 44

The Village (Crabbe) 5, 13, 16, 24, 59, 68, 71, 76, 118, 121–3, 153, 159
  contemporary reception of 58, 69
  dedication 100
  revised version in *Poems* 126
  Samuel Johnson on 60

Wagnerian theory of 'permanent melody' 113
Wallis, Henry 52
Warne, Charles 66
Warwickshire militia 41
Wellington, Duke of 143
Wesley, John 65
Wheble, John 31–2

Whig party and candidates 34, 57, 60, 77–8, 100, 102, 136
Wickhambrook, Suffolk 30
Wickham Market, Suffolk 72
Wilberforce, William 143
Wild, Hans 111
Wilkie, Sir David 137
Williams, Charlotte Campion 147–8, 149–50
Wiltshire 1, 141, 144, 153
  see also Trowbridge, Wiltshire
Winstanley, Rev. Thomas 60
Woodbridge, Suffolk 22, 31, 37, 38, 42, 44, 93, 119
Wordsworth, William 52, 92, 97, 99, 101, 109, 126, 143, 151, 155
workhouse/poorhouse 40–1, 120, 122, 153

yeomanry 19, 44, 45, 146
Yonge, Dr Philip 61
Young, Edward 27–8

You may also be interested in:

Private Lives of the Ancient Mariner:
Coleridge and his Children
by **Molly Lefebure**

In her last published work the celebrated Coleridgean, Molly Lefebure, provides profound psychological insights into Coleridge through a meticulous study of his domestic life, drawing upon a vast and unique body of knowledge gained from a lifetime's study of the poet, and making skilful use of the letters, poems and biographies of the man himself and his family and friends.

The author traces the roots of Coleridge's unarguably dysfunctional personality from his earliest childhood; his position as his mother's favoured child, the loss of this status with the death of his father, and removal to the 'Bluecoat' school in London. Coleridge's narcissistic depression, flamboyance, and cold-hearted, often cruel, rejection of his family and of loving attachments in general are examined in detail. The author also explores Coleridge's careers in journalism and politics as well as poetry, in his early, heady 'jacobin' days, and later at the heart of the British wartime establishment at Malta. His virtual abandonment of his children and tragic disintegration under the influence of opium are included in the broad sweep of the book which also encompasses an examination of the lives of Coleridge's children, upon whom the manipulations of the father left their destructive mark.

Molly Lefebure unravels the enigma that is Coleridge with consummate skill in a book that will bring huge enjoyment to any reader with an interest in the poet's life and times.

'There is a full field of Coleridge scholars at the moment, but in my view Molly was in there first, and is still the outstanding one.' – **Lord Melvyn Bragg**

Molly Lefebure (1919-2013) was a wartime journalist, novelist, children's author, writer on the topography of Cumbria, biographer, and independent scholar and lecturer. She is the author of two other works on the Coleridge family and a volume on the world of Thomas Hardy. *Private Lives of the Ancient Mariner* is the distillation of the lifetime's thought of one who many regard as having been one of the foremost Coleridgean scholars in the world.

First published by The Lutterworth Press, 28 November 2013

Hardback ISBN: 978 0 7188 9300 2
PDF ISBN: 978 0 7188 4189 8
ePub ISBN: 978 0 7188 4190 4

BV - #0008 - 160322 - C4 - 234/156/11 - PB - 9780718896119 - Matt Lamination